The Goal of International Development:
God's Will on Earth, as It Is in Heaven

A Collection of William Carey International University Faculty and Student Writings

Edited by
Beth Snodderly

William Carey International University Press

William Carey International University Press

1539 E. Howard St.
Pasadena, California 91104
Email: wciupress_orders@wciu.edu

Beth Snodderly, Editor
The Goal of International Development: God's Will on Earth, as It Is in Heaven

WCIU Press: International Development Series Number One

Library of Congress Control Number: 2009939350

ISBN: 978-0-86585-027-9

Printed in the United States of America

CONTENTS

DEDICATION

Ralph Winter dedicated the last years of his life to calling attention to the importance of demonstrating the glory of God among all peoples. He saw the field of international development, as practiced by faith-based non-governmental agencies, as a means by which God's people could declare His glory by defeating the works of the devil through acts of loving service. The articles in this book were written and collected before Ralph Winter's death on May 20, 2009, but they represent a tribute to his interests and speculations from the faculty, students, and alumni of the university he founded.

—Beth Snodderly, Editor

INTRODUCTION

Beth Snodderly, Editor

What can committed Kingdom workers do to see God's will done on earth, as it is in heaven? What is the goal of international development? How can globally minded believers demonstrate the character of God while bending their minds to solving the difficult problems of the world? The contributions to this volume by WCIU faculty, students, and alumni approach these questions in a variety of ways.

The Difference Made in the World by People of Biblical Faith

The first three articles look through the lens of global history to see what difference people of biblical faith have made in the world. After an overview by the editor of the big picture of history from the perspective of God's purposes in global history, an article by Chris Teague, a former WCIU student, looks at three views of Old Testament law to see what its significance is for us today in demonstrating God's will. The Old Testament law is full of instructions to Israel for how to do national development—personal, societal, health, sanitation, etc. The principles from God's instructions to Israel should be able to be applied to all other societies throughout the world for diagnosis of what is wrong and principles for how to start getting things right—international development. Being right with God is at the root of the solution in every case, including fighting disease and making the desert blossom like a rose. How did the early believers make a difference when they organized themselves and followed biblical principles? We get a look at the first 100 years of the history of the church in an article by Robert Delgadillo, WCIU's Assistant Vice President for Academic Affairs.

Overcoming Evil

The second set of articles looks more closely at the evil and suffering in this world and the implications for faith-based international development. Due to the activity of the evil one in this world, God's purposes for humankind and creation have been drastically distorted. A short compilation of statements by WCIU Founder Ralph Winter, about the purposes of the Roberta Winter Institute, is the basis for a critique by WCIU student, Willem Zuidema. Although Zuidema agrees that believers are called to combat and correct evils in this world, he is not optimistic that this will lead to widespread transformation of societies. While Zuidema sees the fall of humans as the origin of evil in this world, Winter's autobiographical article, "The Embarrassingly Delayed Education of Ralph D. Winter," outlines the stages in the development of his unique view of the evil one as the root cause of human suffering and societal dysfunction.

The Difference Made by Worldview

One of Winter's most controversial ideas is hard to accept because of the worldview inherited by western Christianty from the Enlightenment philosphers, as David Taylor explains in his article about angelic corruption.

With the reality in mind that people throughout history and around the world are entangled in a web of evil, holding them back from developing into the person or society that God intends them to be, the next two articles look at the difference it can make to follow a worldview that is informed by biblical truths. Doctoral student, Chris Ampadu of Ghana, discusses the negative effect of the worldview of African Traditional Religions on the development of West African societies. His thesis is that this animistic worldview causes Africans to live in the past in which all natural events have already been ordered by the spirits, gods, and ancestors. As a result of this worldview, he concludes, "Africans typically anticipate that grants and aid from the 'advanced countries' are the only hope for our survival." When a society's worldview inhibits it from achieving its God-given potential, there is a need for transformation in the way a people looks at reality. The positive side of the importance of worldview in international development is emphasized in the article by Bruce Graham, WCIU adjunct faculty member. Graham describes how worldview can be transformed through the biblical story.

Intentional Kingdom Breakthroughs

When the worldview of a person or society is in the process of being changed, what does Kingdom mission look like? How does Kingdom work relate to international development? Graham commented in an email conversation with the editor and others in August, 2008, "We've got to nurture a new generation of workers to engage in long term effective cross-cultural efforts to pioneer Kingdom mission efforts in the global south." (The global south is paradoxically both where the largest number of believers and potential Kingdom workers are found, and also where the largest number of unreached peoples are found.) Graham went on to say, "Groups that are sealed off because of culture and language, often in realms of very blatant darkness, because of lack of knowledge and light, need extra effort from people outside 'breaking in' with light. That task does not naturally happen. It requires intentional [organized] effort."

What are some of the skills associated with pioneering breakthrough in various realms of darkness? In the fourth set of articles, the authors present a sample of practical ways in which committed Kingdom workers can share biblical worldview and Kingdom principles that will lead to transformation of people and societies. One means of getting organized for sharing kingdom principles is through the biblical model of house churches, discussed by Don Moon, WCIU doctoral student.

Dave Williams (a pen name), WCIU alumnus, challenges those who wish to be involved in Kingdom mission to allow sending organizations to help them find the place where they can best serve with others to advance the Kingdom. His point is that it is unlikely that an inexperienced new cross-cultural worker will know better than an experienced sending agency where they can have the most impact in seeing a society transformed. As Fred Lewis, WCIU's Vice President for Academic Affairs, said in the email discussion mentioned above, "working towards clean water or more widespread literacy, or evangelism are all good things in themselves individually. But I think God instead has in mind a comprehensive agenda for an entire society. The foundational element in the transformation of a society is whether or not that society is actually following the true God."

What Is the Goal? Two Views

In the last two articles, the authors attempt to define the "goal of international development." A controversial article from Jim Harries, WCIU adjunct faculty member, calls on the body of Christ to consider that the goal of international development from a biblical perspective is the knowledge of and relationship with God. In that case, he suggests, perhaps money, the use of English language in non-western education, and western development activities are not necessary and may even be harmful. Before his death, Ralph Winter, then WCIU Chancellor, commented on this article, "to get people to know God is an ambiguous goal. It should not just mean that poor people at least go to bed knowing that God loves them. The Bible clearly means that we know God well enough to work on His side and to prepare ourselves to fight effectively against the evils of the world and all the things that tear down His glory—and that you can't do by staying in your present fix." Fred Lewis' email comments are also relevant: "I think there is a real difference between 'knowledge of God' and the living out of that knowledge. It is not the case that simply acknowledging the true

God as God 'naturally' leads to societal-wide change. There is a way to live as a society that must be worked out and followed, using biblical principles. Those biblical principles are not limited to what Americans call moral issues. I think that a better way to talk about values is to use the concepts of righteousness, justice and peace. Those biblical principles should be used to deliberately reshape a society's core values and cultural sub-systems so that the whole society in all its parts pleases God."

In the final article, the editor of this volume proposes that the goal of international development, and of the Kingdom of God, is *shalom*—right relationships with God, with other humans, and with God's creation. According to the biblical story, all of these relationships have been corrupted by hideous intentional evil. That means that every believer has a job to do to restore some part of God's creation to God's original design for the world and its inhabitants. Howard Snyder affirms this perspective in his book, *Liberating the Church: The Ecology of Church and Kingdom*: "God's economy is his plan to bring justice, harmony and heath—his perfect *shalom*—to his creation. This he accomplishes through Jesus Christ and the church ... charged with showing forth and helping to bring about God's peace in the ... created world order." (1996, 60)

How can every believing Christian be transformed into a committed Kingdom worker? David Bosch wrote in his book, *Transforming Mission*:

> Those who know that God will one day wipe away all tears
> will not accept with resignation the tears of those who suffer
> and are oppressed *now*. Anyone who knows that one day there
> will be no more disease can and must actively anticipate the
> conquest of disease in individuals and society *now*. And
> anyone who believes that the enemy of God and humans will
> be vanquished will already oppose him *now* in his
> machinations in family and society. (1991, 400)

Ralph Winter often spoke of the importance of every believer needing to know they have a job to do, a war to fight, against the evil one's aggressive attempts to promote the opposite of God's will. Our mission is to defeat evil and restore God's glory. The business of life is to participate meaningfully in this mission and to pray by our actions, "Your Kingdom come, Your will be done on earth as it is in heaven" (Matthew 6:10).

Hopefully, this collection of articles will inspire some serious thinking about specific ways in which individuals can organize themselves to join the Son of God in his mission to "destroy the works of the devil" (1 John 3:8), in this way demonstrating God's original intentions for the earth: right relationships with God, among humans, and with creation.

The views expressed by the writers contributing to this volume are uniquely theirs, offered here as an opportunity for ongoing dialog and learning.

References

Bosch, David J. 1991. Transforming Mission: Paradigm Shifts in Theology of Mission. Maryknoll: Orbis.

Snyder, Howard A. 1996. Liberating the Church: The Ecology of Church and Kingdom. Eugene, OR: Wipf and Stock.

THE BIG PICTURE OF SCRIPTURE

Beth Snodderly

Beth Snodderly is the Provost of William Carey International University and the Coordinator of the Training Division for the Frontier Mission Fellowship, both in Pasadena, California. She studied in the doctoral program of WCIU for 4 years, then completed her doctoral studies in New Testament at the University of South Africa. Her doctoral thesis was written to provide biblical and theological support for Ralph Winter's interpretation of the phrase in 1 John 3:8, "the works of the devil."

The image at the center of First Epistle of John conveys an image that is found throughout Scripture, the cosmic war, the battle for earth: "The Son of God appeared for the purpose of undoing/destroying the works of the devil" (1 John 3:8). From Genesis to Revelation, the consistent theme of Judeo-Christian Scripture is God's purpose to win a people for himself back from the ruler-ship of Satan (see 1 John 5:19: "the whole world lies in the power of the evil one"). This summary of the biblical story presents the big picture of the biblical narrative from the viewpoint of the Johannine community of believers.

A. Big Picture: Prior to the Coming of Jesus

Before the appearing of Jesus, no one had ever seen God (1 John 4:12, John 1:18). The Gospel and First Epistle of John show that God wants to be known to people who choose to be in fellowship with him (1 John 1:3, 4; John 1:12), but the people to whom he chose to reveal himself in most detail, the people of Israel, did not recognize him, in the form of his Son Jesus, when they saw him (John 1:11.) What was blinding and deceiving them, keeping them from recognizing their Creator

(John 1:1-4)? The beginning of Scripture, Genesis 1:1, 2, points to the answer.

The first thing recorded in the Hebrew scriptures, with which the Johannine community would have been very familiar, is that God is having to re-build a world that was in chaos following some sort of disastrous judgment ("*tohu wabohu*").[1] This was apparently due to the sinning of the devil "from the beginning" (1 John 3:8a), prior to the sin of the first humans. Could it be that in an earlier period of time before Genesis 1:1, Satan had turned against God and distorted God's good creation into the suffering and violence now seen throughout nature? According to Genesis 1:26, God created humans to take charge of the creation on his behalf. But at some point the devil, who is a liar and has been a murderer from the beginning (John 8:44), deceived the first humans into joining him in rebelling against God's will. The devil's murderous, hateful nature is illustrated by Cain, who was of the evil one and killed his brother because his deeds were evil, while his brother's deeds were righteous (Genesis 4:3-8; 1 John 3:12). The success of the devil's pervasive influence is seen by the fact that the whole world is said to be under the influence the evil one (1 John 5:19), who is called the "ruler of this world" in John 12:31.

God's plan to reverse the evil one's influence (Genesis 3:15), as recorded in the Penteteuch, called for humans to freely choose to obey him as their rightful ruler. This plan was delayed numerous times by humans making wrong choices and experiencing the consequences, such as the Flood, or when the Israelites asked for a human king and ended up in Exile. Each time judgment was followed by a fresh beginning.

B. Big Picture: Jesus' Life and Death on Earth

Finally, at the right time, God made a radical new beginning: the Word became flesh (John 1:14). John's Gospel is clear that Jesus did not see himself coming to bring further judgment and condemnation, but rather to make eternal life possible for the world God loved so much (John 3:16, 17). Jesus appeared to demonstrate that love, to take away sin and to destroy the works of the devil (1 John 3:5, 8b), loosing people from slavery to sin (John 8:34-36), and making it possible for people to choose obedience to God as their father. (See John 1:12: he gave them the authority or the power to become sons of God.) First John emphasizes two commandments requiring obedience from true children of God: love for one another, and belief in Jesus as the Christ, the Savior of the world (1 John 3:23; 4:14).

The author of 1 John and his inner circle were eyewitnesses that the Father had sent the Son to be the Savior of the world (1 John 1:1-3; 4:9, 14; John 3:16; 4:42). Jesus' ministry began with his baptism by John (1 John 5:6-8; John 1:32-34) and his temptation by the devil, whom he successfully overcame (Matthew 4:10, 11). His ministry included defeating the works of the devil by casting out demons and healing the sick while demonstrating a life of love and obedience to God.

Jesus' life set an example for the believer to follow (1 John 1:7; 2:6; 3:2, 16). His command to his disciples "from the beginning" was to love one another (1 John 4:7, John 13:34, 15:17), one demonstration of which was washing his disciples' feet (John 13:14-16). Not only would his disciples ideally follow his positive example, but they would also experience similar negative consequences. Jesus warned that since the world hated him, it would hate them also (1 John 3:13; John 15:18-24). But the ruler of this world had no hold on Jesus (John 12:31; 14:30) and ultimately will have no hold on Jesus' followers (see 1 John 5:18 which promises that the evil one does not "touch" the believer). Jesus' successful accomplishment of the Father's will led to the driving out and defeat of the evil one. Jesus appeared to take away sins (1 John 3:5) and in doing so, broke the hold that the devil had on humankind (1 John 3:8b; 5:18). Jesus' atoning death on the cross (1 John 2:2) was the turning point in the battle against Satan.

C. Big Picture: After Jesus Returned to the Father

As a result of the devil's works being undone in the lives of Jesus' followers, believers are able and obligated to follow his example by laying down their lives for those in need (1 John 3:16, 17). These demonstrations of love are intended to continue in a chain reaction of destroying the devil's works across time and culture by bringing love where there is hatred (1 John 3:11-17), truth where there is falsehood (1 John 4:1-6), and life to overcome death (1 John 3:14): in other words, God's Kingdom being demonstrated on earth as it is in heaven (Matthew 6:10).

D. Big Picture: The End of History

At the end of the New Testament, in the Book of Revelation, the fulfillment of God's purposes in history is described in terms showing that the state of *"tohu wabohu"* has finally been reversed: there is no more death, crying or pain; and darkness and night have been permanently replaced with "good" light (see Revelation 21:3, 4; 22:5). By describing the opposite of God's intentions in the context of the Creation account, *"tohu wabohu"* points toward the goal of that creation—a place that can be inhabited by humans in purposeful fellowship with God. An adversary that is hostile to life and who opposes God's intentions exists. The biblical story shows humans are to fight back against the enemy who orchestrates disorder and chaos in opposition to God. The rest of Genesis 1 points the way in showing that it is possible to restore order with creativity and patience, showing how to overcome evil with good. John Sailhamer's insight on a play on words illustrates this theme: *"tohu"* describes the land before God made it *"tob,"* good.[2] As believers follow God's and the Son's example, and as they demonstrate what God's will is and what He is like, the peoples of the earth will be attracted to follow that kind of God and experience His blessing.

End Notes

1. The condition of the earth prior to creation is described in Genesis 1:2 as "*tohu wabohu*," which can be translated "destroyed and desolate," or "topsy turvey," or, traditionally, "formless and void." A comprehensive study of the 16 other occurrences of the word, "*tohu*," reveals that the context is judgment on rebellion against God. It seems logical that the first occurrence of the term, in Genesis 1:2, would also have been in the context of judgment, setting the tone for the remaining usages of the term in the Hebrew Bible.

2. J.H. Sailhamer, Genesis Unbound (Sisters, Ore.: Multnomah, 1996), 63.

OLD TESTAMENT LAW: THREE VIEWS

Chris Teague

Chris Teague, a former student in the M.A. program with William Carey International University, is presently working in Central Asia, facilitating incarnational gospel movements through Business As Mission among Muslim Peoples.

The purpose of the Old Testament law given at Sinai is among the most debated themes in systematic theology. The implications of the various conclusions to this debate range from Marcionism,[1] throwing out the entire Old Testament, to Theonomy, setting up the law as the governing moral rule of all civil life. Differing theological systems such as Covenant Theology, Dispensationalism, and everything in between purport different answers to this debate. I am sure that no consensus of understanding on this issue will be reached by the universal church before the second coming of Jesus because we now see in a mirror dimly and know in part. A day is coming when we will see face to face and know fully (1 Corinthians 13:12).

The purpose of this paper is to bring into focus what I believe to be three helpful explanations of the purpose of the Old Testament law from Walter Kaiser, Jr.,[2] Daniel P. Fuller,[3] and John Piper.[4] A clear understanding of these three views should prove helpful in both personal holiness and the task of getting a culturally relevant gospel witness to every tribe, tongue, people, and nation for the glory of God.

Kaiser's View

Kaiser contends that the Old Testament law is a single law with three aspects: moral, ceremonial, and civil (1978, 114). These distinctions, although viewed by many as unbiblical categories are crucial to Kaiser's theory.

1. Moral Law: Universal Principles

Kaiser sees "moral law" as universally applicable to all people in all times and all places. This category is based on Jesus' statement that some parts of the law are weightier than others (Matthew 23:23). Here Jesus is speaking in terms of character over service. Service is expected, but in subordination to character and in the strength that God provides. Therefore, Kaiser feels that the Lord's words indicate some type of ranking or priority within the law. He thus sees the moral law (the Ten Commandments) as a reflection of the character of God and the basis of the civil and ceremonial law (1998, 75). The moral law is, "consequently, the standard of moral measurement in deciding what was right or wrong, good or evil ... fixed in the unwavering and impeccably holy character of Yahweh, Israel's God" (Kaiser 1978, 114). This is therefore the place to turn when we need to know what to do ethically. We learn from the apostle Paul that love is the fulfillment of the law (Romans 13:8-10), but how do we love? The moral law is the ground from which we get the *principles* of how to love. Without it, situational ethics, which often say, "whatever you do, do it in love," can take over and lead to all kinds of embarrassing behavior for the church such as happened in the sixties (Kaiser 1998, 77). The moral law, then, is based on the character of God and is His ethical expectation of His people. The universal principles derived from this underlying foundation are naturally seen in most cultures of the world. For example, murder, theft, rape, lying, dishonoring parents, and dishonoring God or the gods are all perceived to be wrong in the heart of most people in the world. Thus, at least to some level, the law has governed the sense of morality in the world from its inception. This necessarily leads to the subordinate ceremonial and civil laws.

2. Ceremonial Law: A Temporary Pattern

The ceremonial law is usually associated only with the sacrificial system for atonement. However, Kaiser sees the ceremonial law, found mainly from Exodus 25 through Leviticus, consisting of three strands: the sacrificial system, purification rites, and worship, or *the tabernacling of God* (1978, 115-16).

The sacrificial system was put into place with the foreknowledge that man would never be able to keep the infinitely high standards of the moral law. A relationship with God depended on faith in His integrity and ability to be who He claimed to be and do what He promised to do. If man broke the law and sinned, God himself had provided a way to forgive him on the basis of a ransom. Leviticus 17:11 states that the atonement for the souls of men would be through the life blood of an animal. Thus, God provided a way to deal with the surety of man's lawbreaking sin of unbelief (Kaiser 1978, 116).

Kaiser describes the laws of purification as laws of *cleanness*. They were put in place to insure the worshiper was qualified to be in the presence of God. In contrast to cleanliness, cleanness was concerned with a wholeness of heart and behavior rather than the mere external absence of dirt, etc. (1978, 116).

The tabernacling, or dwelling, of God among men was the most important aspect of the ceremonial law. Since there was atonement for sin and a serious mindfulness of the otherness of God expressed through the purification rites, God would now dwell in the midst of His people. This was the main goal of the ceremonial law. However, as Kaiser clearly points out, the ceremonial law was only a foreshadowing of the reality in heaven that was to come (1978, 77-78). It was a temporary pattern which was designed to cease when the reality appeared in Christ.

3. Civil Law: Specific, Practical Application

Kaiser contends that the civil law is the specific, practical application of the moral law. This is where the rubber meets the road in his theory. Kaiser states, "The civil law is an illustration of the principles of the moral law which is found mainly in Exodus 21-23" (1998, 78). The civil law is a guide to help us understand how to live out the moral law. It was not given to frustrate us, but to reduce our difficulties in living out the moral law (Kaiser 1998, 79). It is both particular and specific. Kaiser explains:

> Since the text was given primarily for the common people, the message was relayed on a level where they would find it easiest to grasp. Had the truth been confined to abstract and theoretical axioms, the prerogative would have been confined to the elite and the scholarly. (1987, 155)

Therefore, the moral principles could be applied in many particular ways in the daily affairs of life, depending on the specific situation one was in at the time. Kaiser illustrates by saying that the civil law is to the moral law what case laws are to a judge (1978, 164).

In summary, Kaiser contends that the laws of the Old Testament are fixed in the moral and theological principles of the Ten Commandments. This is consistent with his definition of the moral law as the weightier part of the law of which Jesus spoke in Matthew 23:23. Thus, in principle, he views the Old Testament law as universally binding on all believers today.

Fuller's View

Daniel Fuller's current view of the purpose of the Old Testament law was heavily influenced by one of his students in 1972. During a Greek exegesis course, this student pointed to Romans 9:32 and asked, "How can systematic theology talk of the Old Testament (moral) law as a hypothetical way people could earn their salvation if they complied with it perfectly? This verse makes it very clear that the law does not call for works performed in service for God. Rather, it tells us how we ought to obey God as people who trust His promise to pursue after us to do us good every day of our lives." This question had never occurred to Fuller and he didn't have a satisfactory answer. Consequently, he spent the next fifteen months rethinking his theology on this issue which resulted in his currently held view of the Old Testament law as a law of faith, in contrast to a law of works as held by Calvin (1992, xv-vi). Fuller vehemently contends that the law was never purposed to provide a potential way for Israel to earn or merit her salvation, but consisted of gracious promises of blessing for those who would take hold of them through the obedience of faith (1992, 150-51).

Fuller begins his thesis of the "law of faith" by pointing to the previous commands, with blessings and threats, which God gave to Adam and Eve in the Garden of Eden. He states that Calvin's view of the first sin was one of failure to live up to the standard of meritorious works God had put in place. Disagreeing with this view, Fuller argues that these commands, with their blessings and threats, were not based on a meritorious system, but on faith in the goodness and integrity of God. He contends that the first sin was one of unbelief, or a lack of faith, in God's goodness and integrity to keep His promises (1992, 181). In a sense, these were the "garden laws of faith."

Furthermore, Fuller argues that the Mosaic Laws given at Sinai was also a law of faith. Using Hebrews 4:2, he states that the only reason the law was of no value to Israel is because it was not combined with faith. Considering Galatians 3:21 and Romans 8:3, he concedes that the law itself was deficient in that it did not have the ability to impart life. However, that which kept it from imparting life was the central issue, namely, that God did not accompany it with his heart-regenerating power (1992, 345-46). Therefore, the law itself is good, holy, and able to transform life *when* it is accompanied by the obedience of faith from a regenerate heart. The purpose of the law at Sinai was to show Israel as a whole how sinful they really were by giving them a holy and righteous law without the faith to obey it. The power of the sin of unbelief took hold of the good and righteous law and used it to stir up even more unbelief (1992, 346-47). It illustrated to them how much they really needed the grace and mercy of God. They didn't get it. They turned God's law of faith into a law of works and tried to earn their salvation (1992, 351).

On this basis, Fuller argues that Paul was in no way construing the law in Galatians 3:12, 13 as a law of works. He was arguing against the Judiazer's misinterpretation of the law as a law of works (1982, 200-201). Therefore, he is consistent in his thesis that the law of Moses was a law of faith for the short term purpose of making the sin of unbelief clearer in the Old Covenant and the long term purpose of eternal joy in God through the obedience of faith proceeding from a new heart in the New Covenant.

Piper's View

Piper's current emphasis of the purpose of the Old Testament law has changed over the last 10 years. Piper was the student in Fuller's class who asked the fateful question of the relationship of law and faith in Romans 9:32. Subsequently, both Fuller and Piper held the same view of the law as a law of faith. However, over the last 10 years, Piper's emphasis of the purpose of the law has slightly shifted from a faith-based focus on *law keeping* to a faith-based focus on the *law kept* in Christ. Justification by faith-based *law keeping* or justification by faith in the One who *kept the law* began to be at stake.

1. Law Keeping Focus

Previously, Piper argued that, "the lesson of the whole Old Testament could be summed up in the words of Psalm 37:3, 'Trust in the Lord and do good'" (1995, 150). In other words, the Old Testament law was meant to be fulfilled by an obedience of faith dependent on the moment-by-moment grace of God in contrast to a self-empowered system of works to earn God's favor. The Israelites failed in their pursuit of what the law required because they misconstrued the law as calling for works. They failed to understand the law's call for a life lived by faith in the future grace where God gets the glory for being the gracious provider of the power to obey (1995, 153). This is essentially what Fuller taught. Noticeably, Christ is not mentioned in any of this *law keeping* activity. Thus the question of justification began to arise. At what point is one justified? By what means is one justified?

2. *Law Kept Focus*

Currently, Piper views the purpose of the law in a much more Christ-centric way. He no longer sees the Old Testament law as only teaching obedience through faith, but as demanding a perfect obedience of faith that Israel was to look to Christ to fulfill. God purposely put them under the law to point them to Christ. He argues that the end of the law is Christ in that he perfectly obeyed the law by faith in his Father. Thus, when faith rests on Christ, even in the Old Testament, the record of obedience that he himself lived is reckoned to the believer as righteousness. This is in contrast to faith that simply rested on God to give the grace needed to obey the law. The righteousness of faith-based *law keeping* would never be enough for Israel. Another righteousness was needed, God's righteousness in Christ (Piper 2003). This position brings clarity to the question of justification and puts *law keeping* in subordination to the One who perfectly kept it. The believer is bound to a person, not the law; and *law keeping* is an outworking of justifying faith in the *law kept* by Christ.

The Helpfulness of Each View

The helpfulness of Kaiser's view of the Old Testament law is seen in the universal scope that it provides for guidance and morality. It is more like a way of life based on the character of God that can be integrated into any culture or time. This perspective on the law can help us go a long way in wrestling through moral issues such as abortion, polygamy, etc., that are not clearly spelled out in the New Testament. It is also very helpful as we seek to bring the gospel into very specific cultures with particular practices.

The helpfulness of Fuller's view is in its simplistic challenge of our concept of who God really is and what He expects of us. He is a benevolent God who longs to do His people good by making and keeping very great and precious promises to those who will simply believe what He says and trust Him. It helps us see God as exceptionally loving in contrast to being overbearing and demanding. He does not want us to serve him as if He needed us. He simply wants to make us happy by giving us himself. All He expects of us is faith and the obedience that flows out of it. This is very helpful cross-culturally as we present a God who does not want people to serve His needs, but to wait for Him in faith. This is in stark contrast to every other religious system in the world.

Piper's emphasis on the purpose of the law helps us keep clear that any obedience not resting in Christ's perfect obedience is still legalism, even if it is done in faith. It is helpful because even with our new heart we have such a propensity to turn our focus back to law-keeping instead of fixing our eyes on Christ. It is helpful because every other religion in the world has a default to earn salvation. In keeping justifying faith in the *law kept* in Christ, legalistic synchronism will be better held at bay. Piper's emphasis puts Christ at the center of all of the glory of God and calls us to treasure Him more than anything in the world.

Conclusion

In summary, these three helpful views of the Old Testament law with their particular emphases are yet another display of the grace and kindness of God to help us better understand and apply His Word. The current and continuing debate over the law will most certainly shed more helpful light upon its significance for us today. May we all enter into these discussions with an eye for finding what is useful for building up the saints and expanding the Kingdom of God until the day of its final consummation.

End Notes

1. Marcion was a 2nd century Christian leader and the first person known to have published a fixed collection of books, leading toward the collection we now call the New Testament. He regarded the Old Testament as irrelevant and not authoritative for Christians.

2. Kaiser is a former President and Professor of Old Testament and Semitic Studies at Gordon Conwell Theological Seminary in Boston, Massachusetts.

3. Fuller is the former Dean and Professor of Hermeneutics at Fuller Theological Seminary in Pasadena, California.

4. Piper has been Pastor for Preaching at Bethlehem Baptist church in Minneapolis, Minnesota since 1980. Prior to that he was Associate Professor of Biblical Studies at Bethel College in St. Paul, Minnesota.

References

Kaiser, Walter C. 1978. Toward an Old Testament Theology. Grand Rapids: Zondervan.

______. 1987. Toward Rediscovering the Old Testament. Grand Rapids: Zondervan.

______. 1998. The Christian and the "Old" Testament. Pasadena: William Carey Library.

Fuller, Daniel P. 1982. Gospel and Law: Contrast or Continuum? The Hermeneutics of Dispensationalism and Covenant Theology. Pasadena: William Carey Library.

______. 1992. The Unity of the Bible. Grand Rapids: Zondervan.

Piper, John. 1995. Future Grace. Sisters, Ore.: Multnomah Publishers.

______. 2003. "The Gentiles Have Obtained Righteousness by

Faith." Online. Available from Internet, http://www.desiringgod.org/library/sermons/03/050403.html, accessed November, 2005.

THE DIFFERENCE MADE BY BIBLICAL FAITH IN THE FIRST 100 YEARS C.E.

Robert Delgadillo

Robert Delgadillo is Assistant Vice President for Academic Affairs at William Carey International University. His background as a Catholic scholar working toward a doctorate at an evangelical seminary adds a unique approach to early church history.

Church history is the story of the Christian people. For the individual seeking a deeper understanding of God or a firmer hold onto her or his own faith, there can be a notion of history as only an aggregate of old dates and facts, now long past and largely irrelevant to contemporary faith communities. While history, in itself, is a description of what happens in time and space, history, nonetheless, does tell a story. There is a narrative in history that connects events that reach from the distant past to the present. The history of the church, therefore, provides a narrative of the faith that came to be known as Christianity. Central to the narrative of the Christian church is an assertion of the nature of God. Church history asserts that God acts in time and space, and that human beings can know these actions of God.

The potential for understanding God's actions in history demands a response to the question of how to write about or document these actions for others to understand. The student should not view history as an objective enterprise since there is always the point of view of the historian, whether expressed overtly or covertly, to contend with. At the same time, the reader's careful judgment in discerning history as a subjective narrative should be nurtured. In church history—the living story of the Christian faith—the reader must hold a disposition of both heart and mind toward God, just as the historian did in writing the narrative. It is essential that the student's sensibility be directed toward the movement of God within the inner life of faithful people.

Since church history is the narrative of the Christian people, there is continuity to the events that constitute this history, both forward to the present day and back in time to creation. The challenge is to determine where to begin the narrative. Isolated events do not amount to a narrative; instead church history presents a continuum with God at the fulcrum. Yet, history is not infinite, by definition it is limited by time and space; therefore, a starting point is needed for initiating a discussion or study of the narrative. A key event in the continuum of the history of Christianity can serve this function. At the same time it provides an opening into a method for understanding text. "The world behind the text" becomes a window by which to view the historical, political, cultural, and theological developments that take place while sacred texts, or gospels, were being written. This "world behind the text" allows the contemporary student to begin to understand the ancient world in which the Christian community lived.[1]

Most timelines of Christianity identify the destruction of Jerusalem in 70 C.E. as a pivotal event.[2] Whether the historian or student moves forward or back from that date, the event remains critical to understanding the identity of a Christian and to the religious and cultural movement that took shape in the world of the Gentiles. At the time of Jerusalem's fall, in the Roman Empire there existed a "third race" made up of communities that were neither Jew nor pagan.[3] At the core of the faith within these communities were the four Gospels. These existed in writing by the time of the destruction of Jerusalem. It is no small wonder, then, that the sacred writings of the believers were singled out for confiscation and burning by Roman officials. The persecutors knew the importance of the Gospel texts to the survival of the communities.

The Gospels represented the cumulative written expression of the faith community derisively called "Christians." The origins of these sacred texts were from the memories and oral exchanges that had been passed on from those who had known Jesus to other, younger or newer, members. Many of these new members entering the faith were outside the city of Jerusalem. During the first century, the Roman Empire was a vast expanse. It stretched from Britain to Egypt in the south, and from Spain and northwestern Africa to eastern Anatolia (modern day Turkey) lodging against the Parthian empire. The largest population centers were in the east. While Alexandria was the intellectual locus of the empire and at the same time the third largest city, Jerusalem was at the center of two major trade routes, and held the distinction of being the most populous city in the Roman world.

Within the walls of the great ancient city of Jerusalem the belief in a man named Jesus as Lord spread within the Jewish community at first. This belief in itself was a considerable shift since Jesus of Nazareth had been a Galilean and his ministry had been mostly among the rustic Palestinians. Once the faith moved from the pastoral plains into the urban metropolis its further growth was inevitable. The make up of the believers changed from rural to urban, from uneducated to literate, from speaking Aramaic to Greek speaking. Even so, the cult remained within the religious practices and laws of the Jews. While Jews proselytized Jews, the missionary activity remained mostly within Judaism. However, when the faith reached Jerusalem at the center of the bustling trade routes that moved from north to south and from east to west to all points of the empire, the belief in Jesus the Lord launched a dynamic change.

The urban Jews of the empire were largely assimilated to the language, culture, and even customs of the Hellenized Roman majority. As a consequence, the apostolic missionaries encountered Jews that were not an impoverished group. Instead, they were Greek speaking since they lived mostly outside the Holy Land. Like most immigrant groups, they had left their homeland in pursuit of economic opportunities. They traded and negotiated with non-Jews and these contacts with outside influences made them different from Palestinian Jews. Though many had become successful as merchants and professionals in the urban centers of the empire, they were a large marginalized group that was viewed as neither Greek nor Jew.

It is not surprising, then, that as the belief in Jesus the Lord spread out from Jerusalem the faith would take on characteristics that were particular to each community group. While Jerusalem remained at the center of the faith and dominated in matters of authority and ritual, the ultra-conservative strain of Jewish Christianity that admitted Gentiles into the community demanded full observance of Mosaic Law, including circumcision.[4] To be baptized the believer had to be circumcised (Acts 11:2, 15:5; Gal. 2:3), in other words, become a Jew. Jerusalem still was the center of Judaism, hence also of Christianity, yet outside the walls of the city and perhaps on account of being away from the pious demands of the temple, the practices and stipulations of the belief Jesus is Lord took on variety and differences. James, the brother of Jesus, led a moderate conservative group that insisted that new believers adhere to Jewish observances, except circumcision. The scripture gives an indication of the problems that arose concerning food laws and eating among the uncircumcised (Acts 15:7-12, 15:20; Gal. 2). The distinction in observance among the groups was causing division between the believers fully practicing Jewish customs and those non-Jewish believers unfamiliar with the Mosaic requirements. The insistence of the apostle Paul to preserve the unity of the faithful whenever it was palpably at risk is understandable. As a missionary seeking to hold together his converts, he already sensed the danger of sectarian factions when each believer claimed discipleship to one apostle or another (1 Cor. 1:12).

The missionary endeavors of the early disciples attracted people of all ranks and stations. Even before the destruction of

Jerusalem the faith had extended to other metropolitan centers in the empire. Easy and safe travel throughout the Roman world by way of superior roads or on the sea routes that crossed the Mediterranean, expedited the religious belief in Jesus the Lord to reach the dazzling imperial capital of Rome. Yet the pagan world of the Empire was drawn to a number of Eastern cults.[5] While the Jewish hybrid thrived in Rome, small groups also practiced faiths of eastern origin along with the official Roman religion. Away from the strict authority of the orthodox Jewish sects in and near Jerusalem, the practice of the faith among Gentiles became moderately liberal. The demands for circumcision and kosher dietary restrictions loosened for the newly converted. Baptism, though still obliging a long and difficult process, became easier for non-Jews. Even so, the differences among the groups caused tensions and frictions that threatened the unity of early communities of believers. A fourth group of Jewish believers that followed an ultra-liberal interpretation of the demands on the faithful, saw little or no significance in following the Jewish cult or feasts.[6] The Gospel of John and the Epistle to the Hebrews are the written testaments of this last group.

The four main groups that engaged in most of the missionary activity throughout the Mediterranean world were shocked by the cataclysm that came to Jerusalem in 70 C.E. The Jewish historian Josephus was an eyewitness. He lived in and traveled with the household of the emperor Vespasian and later his son, Titus, and wrote *The Jewish War*. Josephus left a detailed account of the campaigns and battles that culminated in the destruction of Herod's magnificent temple and of the entire city of Jerusalem by the Roman legions. In the seven books that comprise *The Jewish War,* Josephus describes the conquest of Jerusalem. After a number of sieges, Titus, commanding thousands of legionaries, crushed the persistent and increasingly stronger rebellions among the zealous and determined Jewish inhabitants of city. By 70 C.E. the great walls and embankments of Jerusalem and its splendid temple were in ruins.[7] With the destruction of the temple and annihilation of the city, the authority of Jerusalem as the center of Jewish faith and worship ended. Jerusalem also ceased being the nexus of the Jewish-Christian sects. Many communities fled to the safety of Antioch in the neighboring Roman province of Syria. Since about 40 C.E. Jewish missionaries from Jerusalem had been active in converting many other Jews and Gentiles in the large Syrian city (Gal. 2:11-21; Acts 11:19-30). Even so, what happened in Antioch after the fall of Jerusalem became foundational to the history of the church and for the identity of the believing communities. It is in Antioch that the Jewish sects of believers in Jesus the Lord were given the name "Christians" (Acts 11:26). The combination of the destruction of Jerusalem and the taking on of a name for the faith begins a new chapter for Christianity. It marks the end of the first period of the history of the church. Christianity begins it second period.

It is from Antioch that the missions of Paul started and spread throughout the Gentile communities in the Roman Empire. Also from Antioch, the Gospel of Matthew asserted authority through unity. The unity and authority that the evangelist stated in his Gospel coalesced the Christian communities both in the east and in the west and redirected focus to Rome. Missionary zeal became a mandate of the new faith when Matthew added the Great Commission to the end of his Gospel. The threefold order to teach, to baptize, and to disciple are among the important contributions the Antioch community left the church. As unified Christians drew more converts into their community, and as they came to be identified as separate from Jews, their practices and customs began to draw attention. At first neighbors noticed that Christian did not participate in or contribute to pagan festivals. Then the authorities took notice. As early as 64 C.E., Nero ruthlessly persecuted Christians, setting them ablaze as entertainment.[8] It was during this violence in Rome that both Peter and Paul succumbed to the terror inflicted on the first believers. Even before this pogrom, around 49 C.E., the emperor Claudius expelled Jews from Rome because of disturbances regarding the "Chrestos" (Acts 18:2). In the mind of the emperor (and likely in that of most Romans) Jews were the same as Jewish-Christians. In addition to the scriptural reference in Acts, the Roman historian Suetonius also briefly makes mention of it.[9]

Christian faith held a distinct form of worship and a separate identity from its originating Jewish tradition by the end of the first century. Jews and Christians no longer remained the same to the Roman authorities. While the religion of the Jews was sanctioned and recognized, that of the Christians was not. Most pagans began to view the rituals of the Christians as secret and dangerous. In 112 C.E. Pliny the Younger, a historian then serving as the Roman governor of Bithynia in Turkey, writes to the emperor Trajan expressing a concern for tales of cannibalism, incest, and treason. These charges arose on account of the Christian practice at Communion to take the "blood" and "body" of Christ; the profession of "love" for "sisters and brothers"; and for the Christian refusal to worship the emperor.[10] Pliny notes that "the usual result of spreading the crime" occurs despite the persecution and death he brought to the Christians that refused to renounce their belief after being asked three times. Furthermore, in his letter to Trajan he accounts that "many persons of every age, of every rank, of both sexes even, are daily involved."[11] The Christian faith was growing not only in numbers, but also in determination and boldness. Two generations after the crucifixion, believers were willing to die for their faith in Jesus Christ.

Though Roman persecution was at times tolerant of the Christians, Jewish hostility grew after the destruction of Jerusalem. Christians were rarely allowed to preach in synagogues. As a result, worship for Christians took place in private homes. Moreover, in contrast to pagans, the Christians began to be recognized for their steadfast moral convictions. Despite Pauline exhortations that indicate the contrary in Corinthians, Christians aspired to a high moral and ethical code. Roman authorities and common pagan society noted that Christians appealed to a higher moral character on account of the transformation that the Gospel brought to them. As a result, Christians helped one another, and they sought fellowship with those of different traditions or customs. In sharing the Gospel, they made peace with those who hated them or who persecuted them, and promised new believers a joyful reward from God.[12] Yet ignorance about and suspicion of Christians persisted. They became easy targets of violence and the suspects of many crimes. On account of their allegiance to Jesus Christ as *Kurios,* or Lord, who ruled over the whole earth, Christians faced the serious charge of subversion of the state. They were seen as transgressors of the laws that upheld the authority and the religious cult of the emperor. Christians that persisted in their faith, despite repeated opportunities to recant, were subject to execution. It is not surprising, consequently, that the Christian communities of the Roman Empire suffered ten major persecutions in a period of about two hundred and fifty years. The attempts to purge the empire of the growing Christian numbers can be sorted into two main chronological groups.[13] The first set of persecutions began under Nero in 64 C.E. and lasted until about the year 250. They were mostly local and did not result in massive loss of life. The second wave was relentlessly and viciously carried out throughout the Empire as the Roman authorities intended to rub out Christianity as a grave threat to the power of the state. The early persecutions of Christians included the violent one ordered by the emperor Domitian (51–96 C.E.), who proclaimed himself lord and god. He was indiscriminate in killing those who would not proclaim his deity, whether they were Christian, Jew, or even his own family members. It was during his short but bloody reign that the Christian communities encountered the events that formed the basis for the Book of the Apocalypse (Rev. 17: 5,6) *The Revelation of John,* the New Testament's last book and probably written much later than Nero in 95 C.E., remains a scriptural testimony of the horrors that Rome inflicted on the Christian believers (Rev. 17).

Persecutions under various emperors would continue for nearly 300 years until Constantine endorsed the Christian faith as the official religion of the Roman Empire. During this long period of the formation of Christian identity, believers were often willing to die rather than to recant their faith. In the end, the patient and persistent faith of followers of Jesus overcame the worst of what the Roman government could do, resulting in a society adopting principles of biblical faith as its normative law.

This segment of the history of the church is only a portion of the total narrative that could be told. The formulation of what constituted true and false belief about God, rules for dealing with heretics and those who denied Christ under pressure of persecution, and the practical details of church governance were all yet to come. But the theme of obedient faith and the difference this eventually makes in a society influenced by groups of committed believers in Jesus is a common thread throughout the history of the Christian church.

End Notes

1. For a full explanation of this methodology see Sandra M. Schneiders, The Revelatory Text: Interpreting the New Testament as Sacred Scripture (Collegeville, Minn.: Liturgical Press, 1999), 113. In the system introduced by Schneiders to interpret sacred text, she identifies three "worlds": the world behind the text; the world of the text; and the world before the text.

2. C.E. means "Common Era," a chronological designation that is acceptable to non-Christians. It replaces A.D., meaning *Anno Domini*, or "Year of Our Lord." The corresponding designation for the earlier period is B.C.E. It means "Before Common Era," which replaces B.C., or "Before Christ."

3. Brian Moynahan, The Faith: A History of Christianity (New York: Doubleday, 2002), 44.

4. Raymond E. Brown and John P. Meier, Antioch and Rome: New Testament Cradles of Catholic Christianity (New York: Paulist Press, 1983), 2-6. In the introduction of this book, Brown identifies four main groups of Jewish missionary believers.

5. Moynahan, The Faith, 28. Isis from Egypt was worshipped as far as the Rhine; Cybele, the Great Mother cult from Asia Minor, had a temple on the Palatine Hill. Military officers in Rome worshipped the Persian sun god Mithras at about the same time as the crucifixion. Even the emperors practiced the cult well into the third century.

6. Brown asserts that missionary efforts of the different groups often overlapped. Therefore, an ultra-conservative group could proselytize a group converted by more liberal group and vice versa (Antioch and Rome, 6).

7. Moynahan. The Faith, 43.

8. Writing fifty years after the event, Tacitus in his Annals describes how Nero blamed the Christians for igniting the great fire that nearly destroyed Rome. The emperor had deemed the Christians easy victims to blame in an effort to squelch the dangerous rumor that the fire had been set at his orders. After describing the brutality of the terror inflicted on the Christians, Tacitus notes that the mob took pity on them and turned against Nero.

9. Suetonius. De Vita Caeaerum, 5.25.4.

10. Moynahan. The Faith, 51.

11. Moynahan. The Faith, 52.

12. Kenneth Scott Latourette, A History of Christianity: Beginnings to 1500, revised ed. (Peabody, MA: Prince Press, 2003), 84

13. Latourette, History of Christianity.

References

Alison, James. 2003. Raising Able: The Recovery of the
    Eschatological Imagination. New York: Crossroad
    Publishing Co.

Donovan, Mary Ann.

______. 2002. "Church to 1400: HS2498." Course Lectures,
    Jesuit School of Theology, Berkeley, California, September 3
    to October 3.

Irenaeus. 1989-1994. Against Heresies. In Ante-Nicene Fathers:
    The Writings of the Fathers Down to AD 325, edited by
    Alexander Roberts and James Donaldson, 414-429. Grand
    Rapids: Eerdmanns.

Latourette, Kenneth Scott. 2003. A History of Christianity:
    Beginnings to 1500. Revised ed. Peabody, MA: Prince Press.

Moynahan, Brian. 2002. The Faith: A History of Christianity.
    New York: Doubleday.

New Advent Catholic Encyclopedia. n.d. www. newadvent.org,
    [accessed December 22, 2008].

Rye, Jesse. n.d. "Greek Masks."
    http://www.ripon.edu/Academics/Theatre/THE231/RyeJ
    /Masks/site/home.html (accessed December 22, 2008].

Schneiders, Sandra M. 1999. The Revelatory Text: Interpreting
    the New Testament as Sacred Scripture. 2nd ed. Collegeville,
    MN: The Liturgical Press.

Sheerin, Daniel J. 1986. The Eucharist, (Message of the Fathers of
    the Church), v. 7. Wilmington, DE: Michael Glazier.

THE PURPOSES OF THE ROBERTA WINTER INSTITUTE

Ralph D. Winter with Beth Snodderly

Ralph D. Winter was the founder and former president of William Carey International University. He was serving as Chancellor at the time of his death on May 20, 2009. He is considered by the evangelical world to be one of the foremost missionary statesmen of the 20th century.

The Roberta Winter Institute will try to upgrade our desire to bring glory to God by ending our apparently neoplatonist truce with Satan in the realm of all his ingenious and destructive works. Our global mission agencies, which already have to their credit the discovery of the nature of leprosy, will declare war on other sources of disease in addition to being kind helpfully to sick people and preaching resignation amidst suffering.

Mobilized Christian response did not come soon enough to materially help my wife, and may not help you or yours. But the least we can do is set something in motion that may rectify our understanding of a God who is not the author of the destructive violence in nature and who has long sought our help in bringing His kingdom and His will on earth.

We Are in a War against an Intelligent Enemy

What I am trying to do, groping into it gradually but as fast as I can, is to try to undo a huge and diabolical complex of misunderstandings which enervates and destroys any resistance we might offer to the distorting works of the Devil. My pastor (Gordon Kirk, Lake Avenue Congregational Church in Pasadena, California) who is a former theology professor at Biola has observed that "Satan's greatest achievement has been to cover his tracks." This urges us to recognize that we are extensively unaware of diabolic activity in the world.

In scripture we see the prominence of the emphasis on the coming of God's Kingdom, and note that "the Son of God appeared for this purpose, to destroy the works of the Devil (1 John 3:8)." What if all disease pathogens as well as all violent forms of life are the work of Satan? How would that amplify and refocus our global mission?

When Satan turned against God precisely what kind of destruction and perversion did he set out to achieve? Where would we see evidence of his works? Would he set out to pervert the DNA of originally tame animals? Would he employ powers of deception so that we would get accustomed to pervasive violence in nature and no longer connect an intelligent evil power with evil and suffering? Worse still, would Satan even successfully tempt us to think that God is somehow behind all evil— and that we must therefore not attempt to eradicate things like smallpox lest we "interfere with Divine Providence"?

In the last 20 years paleontologists have dug up more evidences of earlier life forms than in all previous history. One of their thought-provoking discoveries is that pre-Cambrian forms of life revealed no predators. Then, at that juncture destructive forms of life suddenly appeared at all levels, from large creatures to destructive forms of life at the smallest microbiological level. Is this what Satan set out to do from the time he fell out with the Creator—that is, did he set about to pervert and distort all forms of life so as to transform all nature into an arena "red in tooth and claw" that reigns today?

We need to recognize and ponder more seriously the kind and degree of harm Satan is able to cause. We need to unmask the works of Satan. Are we fellowships of survivors or of soldiers? We are all enlisted to war against the works of Satan.

Attributing Evil to God/Distortion of God's Character

There are very many people, even Bible-believing Christians, not just non-Christians, who are profoundly puzzled, perplexed, and certainly confused by the extensive presence of outrageous evil in the created world of all-powerful, benevolent God. In coping with this, they may frequently attribute to God what is actually the work of an evil intelligence, and thus fatalistically give not the slightest thought to fighting back.

The assumption that all evil comes from God is pagan, coming from neo-Platonism which taught there is one God who is the source of both evil and good. We have inherited this thinking in our view of Romans 8:28. The Intelligent Design people don't take into account that they are attributing the creation of evil to God. Darwin did not do this. Instead he invented the wacky theory of unaided evolution. But Darwin at least recognized the presence of evil if not intelligent evil, and even the need to protect the reputation of a benevolent God. In that, he scored higher than what we see in the written materials of Intelligent Design.

The corollary to this mistaken assumption that all evil comes from God is that we can't go after evil because we'd be going after God. The pattern is to be "resigned" to evil, even to presume that God is behind all things rather than that God is in front of all things, turning Satanic evil into good, but by no means initiating the evil, much less suggesting that we do nothing about it.

Free Will/God Works through Intermediaries

We need to recognize the very radical and significant decision of God to create beings, angelic and human, with true free will and to work through those intermediaries. We may frequently ask God to do things which He has been expecting us as intermediaries to do. Our mission then may need to include things for which we ordinarily only pray.

The Concept of Inappropriate Prayer

This is seldom discussed in Evangelical circles. As a result, we fail frequently to distinguish between what part God wants us to play and what part only He can play. Confusion in this area is clearly in Satan's favor. He is glad when he can get us to ask God to do something God expects us to do. But it must be true that God empowers those who seek him and want to do His will.

We don't ask God to paint the back fence.

We don't ask God to evangelize the heathen (as they did in William Carey's day).

We should not ask God to take care of disease.

God, we know, invites us to bind up the wounds we can see with our eyes and to ward off evil which is large enough to see without a microscope, but He also has seemed to want to await human collaboration in fighting the microbiological roots of evil for some reason we may not fully understand. We have an un-updated theology, thinking that we aren't responsible to do something about something we can't see (microbes). But we CAN see these now and do something. We are casting aside a whole arena of responsibility.

Theologizing the Microbiological World

It seems likely that now that we have new knowledge about the outside sources of several massive diseases that we cannot in good conscience fail to do what we can to mount new offensive warfare with those attacking sources.

Our theologies, that is, our formalized ways of attempting to think biblically, were hammered out during centuries that were totally blind to the microscopic world. Evangelicals have recently stressed the inevitable intelligence and design in nature, but they have not, to my knowledge, attempted to suggest that there is evidence of any evil intelligence and design. This is perhaps due to a theological tradition which does not understand demonic powers to have the ability to distort DNA. Our Evangelical theological tradition is so old that it also would not conceive of good angels working at the DNA level. In other words, we have no explicit theology for intentional modification of either good or bad bacteria. Our current theological literature, to my knowledge, does not seriously consider disease pathogens from a theological point of view—that is, are they the work of God or Satan? Much less does this literature ask the question, "Does God mandate us to eliminate pathogens?"

Discover and Eradicate the Origins of Disease Rather than Treatment and Prevention

Surprising recent insights show that many diseases are basically caused by outside invaders which we need to fight in the same sense as we fight the crime of visible terrorists. Does nutrition, exercise, banishing anxiety, etc. protect you or cure you of Malaria? Are our immune systems normally capable of defeating Malaria, Tuberculosis, Smallpox, Anthrax, etc.? No, not normally. And, if the latest thinking is correct, slow-acting viruses underlie heart disease as well as cancer, multiple sclerosis, Alzheimer's, and Schizophrenia.

So, do we go on just praying in addition to making sure we heed these other things (nutrition, exercise, peace of soul and mind, etc.)? It is understandable, of course, that we would not automatically think about going beyond prayer and taking concrete measures to quell the source of these destructive diseases if we did not know that they are caused by attacking pathogens which our immune systems, no matter how healthy, cannot always overcome.

I recently spent a couple of hours prayerfully perusing a book that patiently, in great detail, describes how over 200 years of early Spanish missionary work went down the drain. The word "Florida" in the 16th century included not only our present state by that name but also the entire southeast of the USA, in the triangle from Virginia to Alabama to Miami. In that area lived literally hundreds of thousands of Native Americans.

Well, between about 1530 and 1800 primarily Spanish work was undertaken employing both soldiers and priests, the latter very faithfully. Lots of good things and unwise things happened, but eventually "missions" (outposts) of the kind we see still standing in California, 150 of them, were planted. Each one was a worship center, an educational center, and an industrial center. However, today there is not a physical trace of a single one of those painstakingly established missions. Worse still, the entire Indian population, as in Cuba, has totally vanished, dying primarily of European diseases.

All of those hundreds of thousands of people! Their religion certainly did not save them, at least not in this life. I admit that I cannot easily shake off the sensation of strangeness and tragedy hovering over those 250 years during which Spanish, French and British fought each other and in some cases Indian uprisings, without realizing that their real and common enemy was Satanically devised pathogens.

Implications for Cross-Cultural Work: Bringing Glory to God

Are we to send people to represent Christ around the world simultaneously to implant disease and offer eternal salvation? You will say no, not intentionally. But what about the diseases they already have? Are we to help them to eradicate those diseases (not just be kind to those who get sick)?

To destroy the works of the devil is one major way in which our testimony of word and deed can glorify the true nature of our living God, our heavenly father. It is not an alternative to evangelism, it will make our evangelism more credible. It is to rectify our God's damaged reputation. It is to avoid extending the implicit and embarrassing policy of almost constantly misrepresenting Him in our work around the world. Attacking the roots of disease is part and parcel of our basic mandate to glorify God in all the earth.

The principal concern in all of this is the distortion we can see in many people's ideas of God. Pause and consider Tozer's statement that "The most important thing about you is what comes to your mind when you think of God." Our theological inheritance was hammered out before germs were known of. A full awareness of the larger scope of the battle against God is not yet ours. In regard to horrifying violence in nature, people have become so used to it, so accustomed to it, so hardened to it, so calloused about it that they have drifted into suppositions that this must be the way God created things. (Only Satan is happy about that.) And, people get to thinking that a God who does not mind violence, cruelty and suffering, whether among animals or man, is not the most appealing kind of a God when we set out to win people to Christ, His Son.

The Purpose for the Roberta Winter Institute

At this point it is time to ask the question why it is that the mounting muscle of the very considerable movement of all those globally who are moved by Jesus Christ has not weighed in either theologically or practically in the area of working to correct distortions of nature and of God's will by going to the roots of the problem. In a way this is the most ominous fact of all. I know of no theological tradition, no denomination, no Christian school—or hospital for that matter—that has seriously accepted the roots of the challenge of the enormous and continuing and growing factor of disease in this world of ours.

Meanwhile constantly both believers and non-believers are stumbling about wondering over the amount, the harshness, and the unpredictability of evil in our world. Indeed, the credibility of an all-powerful and loving God is constantly being called into question by people who are no longer content to suppose "that God has His reasons." We may indeed not know all His reasons. But do we have reasons for our inaction?

It is truly astonishing how much greater we can make the impact of our evangelism if the true spectrum of concern of our loving God is made clear and is backed up by serious attention not only to treating illness but to eradicating the evil causes, the works of the devil. Gordon Kirk says that "Satan's greatest achievement is to cover his tracks." That, surely, is why we get out of practice speaking of him or recognizing his works or even recognizing his existence. Yet, when we reinstate his existence as an evil intelligence loose in God's creation only then do a lot of things become clear and reasonable. Otherwise God gets blamed for all kinds of evil: "God took my wife," etc.

I find it difficult, after making this switch, not to conclude that Satan's angels are the source of life-destroying forms of life, vicious animals, bacteria, viruses. Not that he created them but that he tampered with their DNA to distort them. To "destroy his works" means thus to take it as part of our efforts, our mission, to glorify God to restore, with God's help, what Satan has distorted. Thus, you see the rationale for establishing the Roberta Winter Institute.

The primary focus of this new institute will not be laboratory science but public and mission awareness of the need for a new theological sensitivity for destroying the works of the devil.

A Response to Ralph Winter's Rationale for the Roberta Winter Institute

Willem Zuidema

Willem Zuidema is a graduate student with William Carey International University who has been active with the ships ministry of Operation Mobilization. This article is a condensed version of an Integrative Paper Zuidema wrote in fulfillment of requirements for the M.A. program.

The main issues raised by Ralph Winter in his statements about the purposes of the Roberta Winter Institute can be summarized as the origin of evil and the meaning of salvation. The thesis of this paper is that the origin of evil is a mystery, but somehow related to the fall of mankind. The goal of salvation in Christ is not simply "to fit individuals for heaven," but for God to create "a people for his name;" an eschatological people, who together by the power of the Spirit live the life of the future in the present age as they await the final consummation (Fee 1996, ix).

Winter's thinking may be helpfully compared with that of N.T. Wright in his analysis of The Gospel of Judas, a writing of early Gnostics. A main charge of both Winter and Wright is that, in the course of time and in the process of communicating the Gospel, ideas that are foreign to Scripture, coming from neo-Platonism and neo-Gnosticism, have entered modern evangelicalism, resulting in a dualistic attitude towards creation and a lack of involvement in community work at large (Wright) and medical work at the grassroots level in particular (Winter).

With Winter and Wright, I will argue that the Christian Church needs to get (more) involved in community development work. Against Winter, I would not attribute all life-destroying life forms to the devil. Whereas with Wright I affirm that salvation involves the restoration of all things and that "living the life of the future" includes an expectation to participate "in the coming restoration of all things," I am less optimistic than he is in my expectation to see transformed societies resulting from the impact of cross-cultural evangelism.

Winter states that "the primary focus of the Roberta Winter Institute will be to raise public and mission awareness of the need for a new theological sensitivity for destroying the works of the devil." Because most of our theology was formed before there was any knowledge of the microscopic world, the works of the evil one at this level have gone unnoticed. By attributing all things—including evil—to God, the Church has adopted a pagan (neo-Platonist) view which has resulted in a fatalistic attitude. Winter recognizes that whereas evangelicals have recently stressed the inevitable intelligence and design in nature, he states that they have not acknowledged the evidence of evil intelligence and design. At least Darwin, in spite of his faulty theory of unaided evolution, recognized the presence of evil in creation and the need to protect the reputation of a benevolent God. The latter is exactly what (modern) evangelicals have failed to do and Winter argues that mission work that includes scientific work in the field of medicine will "rectify our God's damaged reputation." It is not an alternative to evangelism, but makes our evangelism more credible and is part of our mandate to bring glory to God. As a result of the work of the Roberta Winter Institute, Dr. Winter hopes that faith-based NGOs will get involved in the fight against all sources of disease in addition to helping sick people and preaching resignation amidst suffering.

Winter and Wright have in common that they charge modern evangelicalism with having adopted ideas that are pagan rather than scriptural. Interestingly they go separate paths to arrive at similar conclusions and practical implications. On the one hand Winter argues that the Church has adopted a form of neo-Platonism by attributing evil to God, resulting in a fatalistic attitude and lack of willingness to attempt to eradicate diseases "lest we interfere with Divine Providence." Wright, on the other hand, argues that the modern evangelical attitude towards creation is dualistic and escapist (and therefore can be characterized as neo-Gnostic). Likewise this has resulted in a lack of involvement in society and lack of motivation to bring about the signposts of the coming of the Kingdom.

Winter is specific in the cause that he would like to see addressed (disease pathogens), as well as his reasons: they are caused by Satan and therefore, as part of the missionary mandate, the Church is called to fight them, which will bring greater glory to God and make evangelism more credible. Wright does not give specific examples of causes that should be dealt with by Christians.

Both articles deal with our eschatological hope. Wright is explicit in his statement that the goal of 'salvation' (clearly in its widest sense, not referring to an individual's salvation) is the remaking of the good God-given created universe and our future hope is the participation in that restored universe. That same thought seems to underlie Winter's article when he says that "to destroy his [Satan's] works means to take it as part of our efforts, our mission, to glorify God to restore, with God's help, what Satan has distorted."

The Origin of Evil

Ralph Winter concludes that Satan and his angels are the source of life-destroying form of life, vicious animals, bacteria, viruses. Not that they created them, but they tampered with their DNA to distort them. This conclusion should be qualified and some of Winter's arguments are weak. He states that our theological tradition does not understand demonic powers to have the ability to distort DNA. The question is, do they? Winter calls the fact that pre-Cambrian forms of life revealed no predators thought-provoking. That is true, but not necessarily in the sense that he means. This argument carries the suggestion that Satan's rebellion occurred in the pre-Cambrian period. The pre-Cambrian period is the eon from about 3,800 million years ago until 544 million years ago. This is of course long before human beings appear. Regardless of which view one holds with regard to the creation account in Genesis 1, the fact is that after creating human beings God still calls creation "very good" (Gen. 1.31) and there is no suggestion that the Satan's rebellion had taken place and / or had resulted in distortion of creation (even at DNA level). Actually up until the point that Satan first appears in the Genesis account (as the serpent of Gen. 3.1) there is no indication that anything is wrong. Now this is thought provoking, not to say puzzling, because as Winter points out, paleontologists have shown predators to appear long before that. Unless one reads Genesis 1 literally and holds to a "24-hours-view" (and basically denies merit to most paleontological and other scientific findings), it seems to show God as the Creator of those first predators and therefore that physical death was part of God's good creation. According to Dwight Baker, Gnosticism is an attempt "to remove from God .... the stigma of creation." (Baker 1998: 61-3). This was done of course by assuming that the universe was made by a "lesser god", the demiurge. Baker continues and says that in a sense, neo-Platonism, represented by Plotinus, did the same by creating "enough distance between the One (God) and the material world so that God wasn't responsible for the material world."

Evaluation

These attempts by neo-Platonism and Gnosticism show the depth of the problem, but attributing all evil to Satan does not solve it either. Biblical demonology was only fully developed during and after the Babylonian exile. Scripture reflects the fruit of Jewish theological reflection that was induced by their exposure to Zoroastrian thought. Whereas later biblical revelation seems dualistic and shows Satan and his demons as God's adversary (and the spiritual warfare that is involved in the implementation of God's Kingdom) that should always be understood in light of the earlier revelation that shows him as subject to God (Job 1.6–2.7) and even as one of God's instruments (Exodus 12.12, 13, 23). If one point stands out from Isaiah 40–48, it is God's absolute sovereignty. Even where it is said of the devil that he holds the power of death (Hebrews 2.14), that should be understood in light of Job 2:6 where God does not allow Satan to take Job's life.

Until Genesis 3, God's creation was good and had not been affected by evil. Evil was the result of mankind's fall, which affected the whole universe. Creation itself is subjected to frustration, in bondage to decay, eagerly awaiting for the sons of God to be revealed and right up to the present time groaning as in the pains of childbirth (Romans 8.19-23). Comfort (1993: 322) confirms that creation's fall was the result of humanity's disobedience as steward of creation. Therefore it should be concluded that ultimately disease and suffering are consequence of mankind's sin. That is not to say that some diseases are not directly caused by Satan and his demons. Scripture testifies to that as well (Mt 9.32-33; Mt 12.22-23; Lk 13.10-17). These are all cases of demon-possession though and dealt with accordingly, i.e., through Jesus' direct engagement of demons to set people free. (Moreau 2000: 267)

Although it is fair to conclude that Satan's evil designs have always been subject to God's sovereignty (e.g. Moreau 2000: 268 and McRay 2000: 853), we are left with the mystery. And how puzzling and disconcerting it is follows from men's numerous attempts to explain evil. The concepts of good and evil and explanations about the origin of evil are present in (and often central to) many religious and philosophical systems.

The two systems mentioned by Winter and Wright (neo-Platonism and Gnosticism respectively) deal with the origin of evil in their own ways, but as mentioned above they both somehow try to remove the responsibility for the creation, or at least the presence of evil in creation, from God. According to Ferguson (1993: 367-69), neo-Platonism was created by Plotinus (205–270 C.E.) and had an enormous influence on Christian thought (through Origin, the Cappadocians, and Augustine). It consisted of Platonism with Aristotelian, Stoic, and Neopythagorean elements. Most important for our study is that neo-Platonism maintains Platonic dualism (even though expressed within a framework of ultimate unity—the One) and that it denies the existence of evil: "Evil is not an ontological reality. Nothing is evil in its nature. Evil is nonbeing, the term of limit of being." (Ferguson 1993: 369) It is this latter conviction that must have motivated Winter to compare the thinking of many Christians with neo-Platonism, and call it pagan. Perplexed by the presence of evil in the created world of all-powerful, benevolent God, Christians have not only attributed evil to God, but in doing so have practically denied the existence of evil all together. As shown above, attributing all evil to the devil is not the biblical solution. Rather creation's fall was the result of mankind's fall and, as should be added, the devil has taken advantage of it. Therefore, with Winter, the fatalistic attitude and the lack of willingness to "fight back" that may result from attributing evil to God are to be avoided.

Gnostics attempted to avoid attributing evil to God, as exemplified in the Gospel of Judas, through a dualistic worldview of a transcendent God and an ignorant demiurge. The material world created by this demiurge, which included the body, was regarded as inherently evil. Most Gnostics denied Christ's incarnation and advocated special secret knowledge for the initiated. N.T. Wright was one of the first to refute the teachings of the recently discovered Gnostic Gospel of Judas. In his sermon "As One Who Serves," published on his home page, Wright explains that Gnostic thinking came about as a result of the mentality that the world and its power-structures were irredeemable and that the proper attitude towards it was one of escapism into one's private spirituality, which ended up in going after another god (the demiurge, the inferior creator-god). Documents were created in which the Jesus story was presented as if Jesus himself had taught these ideas and that his "true message was helping us to discover who we really are." This idea appeals to the modern mind as well and it has become, in Wright's words, "a major if not the major alternative, in the popular mind, to the true path of the kingdom." Wright further points out however that this Gospel of Judas has no historical value (it teaches nothing about the real Jesus and Judas), it offers a worldview that is opposed to the biblical one, and, as such, it takes away the motivation "to work for God's kingdom in the real world." And this is where Wright's main concern lies, namely with the fact that dualistic (Gnostic) thinking has entered the evangelical mind as well and that has resulted in a widespread "dualistic spirituality and escapist soteriology." In Gnosticism the means of salvation was "knowledge." The goal of salvation was for the spark of the divine, which was planted in some souls, to escape out of the material world. Gnosticism adopted an "anti-cosmic" stance, with a thoroughly negative evaluation of the material world. (Ferguson 1993: 290)

The Kingdom of God

Both Winter and Wright make reference to the Kingdom of God, without specifying their position on the millennium. Wright's statement that "[the Messiah's message] ... compels the followers of Jesus, energized by the power of his Spirit, to go out into the world and make new creation happen," as well as his expectation to see "changed lives and societies in the present time," seems overly optimistic, similar to a post-millennium viewpoint. However, Wright does qualify that he recognizes that there will be partiality and ambiguity due to the already/not yet nature of the Kingdom in its present form. Although a society should experience the positive influence of a believing community of transformed individuals in its midst, I believe that to expect transformation of society at large is unrealistic. One should also ask whether "war on …sources of disease" that Winter advocates and the involvement in "the world of politics and society" (Wright) will be seen as signposts of the Kingdom. Winter claims that the nature of leprosy was discovered by global mission agencies, but is that seen as a signpost of the Kingdom by any unbeliever?

The true signpost of the Kingdom is the church, the community of believers, who by the power of the Spirit live a Kingdom life. God takes a people for himself (Acts 15.14), to dwell in their midst (1 Cor 3.16; Rev 21.3), and by his presence to empower them to be Christ's witnesses (Acts 1.8). Compelled (and empowered!) by the Spirit one can get involved in medical or other social community work, but these should be seen as acts of love and compassion, and as such, yes, signposts of the Kingdom. Medical work engaged in by cross-cultural workers (and especially where that has not yet happened, at the roots of the problem, i.e. the sources of disease) is necessary and will impact society and to a degree transform it. But, as David Dockery puts it, "it is the responsibility of the Church to work for and pray for peace and justice on earth, but ultimate peace and justice are precluded by the sinfulness of humanity." (1992: 839) It is exactly this recognition of "partiality and ambiguity" (to use Wright's own words as quoted above) that are not sufficiently present in either Wright's or Winter's articles.

Conclusions

The community of the redeemed is the real signpost of the Kingdom in its witness to Christ in word and deed. The word is the proclamation of the Gospel. The deeds are the fruit and gifts of the Spirit, as well as the "good works which God prepared in advance for us to do" (Eph. 2.10). The community of the redeemed is called to fight against and undo the results of the fall and thus bringing glory for God. For the local church that means being involved in all kinds of community development projects to which God has called and equipped it.

But in line with my argument, we should not be overly optimistic with regard to its effects. In spite of all our intellectual and technological progress, man is still morally flawed and in need of personal transformation by the power of the Gospel and the Spirit.

I do not want to deny the importance and necessity of community development work or deny its impact on culture, but many wonderful social, educational and medical projects have been set up and carried out by unbelievers. By way of contrast, our righteousness and our "acts of righteousness" should surpass those of the world (Mt. 5.20; 6.1). It is the light of the presence of Christ that should "shine before, that they may see our good deeds and praise our Father in heaven" (Mt. 5.16). Only then will people: "see and know, ... consider and understand, that the hand of the Lord has done this, that the Holy One of Israel has created it." (Isaiah 41.20)

References

Baker, Dwight P. 1998. "Religious and Political Developments in the Roman World." Global Civilization: Lesson Overviews. William L. Osborne and Ralph D. Winter, eds. Pasadena: William Carey Library.

Comfort, P.W. 1993. "Futility." In Dictionary of Paul and His Letters. Gerald F. Hawthorne, Ralph P. Martin, and Daniel G. Reid, eds. Downers Grove: InterVarsity Press.

Dharmajah, Premkumar. 1998. "Reflections on Hinduism." Ancient World Reader, 2nd ed., vol. 2, William L. Osborne and Ralph D. Winter, eds. Pasadena: William Carey Library.

Dockery David S. 1992 . "Christian Faith and the Christian Community." In Holman Bible Handbook. David S. Dockery, ed. Nashville: Holman Bible Publishers.

Drummond, Richard. 1994. "The Buddha's Teaching." In Eerdmans' Handbook to the World Religions. Pat Alexander, ed. Grand Rapids: Eerdmans.

Fee, Gordon D. 1996. Paul, the Spirit, and the People of God. Peabody, MA: Hendrickson.

Ferguson, Everett. 1987. Backgrounds of Early Christianity. Grand Rapids: Eerdmans.

McRay, John. 2000. "Satan." In Evangelical Dictionary of World Missions. A. Scott Moreau, Harold Netland, and Charles van Engen, eds. Grand Rapids: Baker.

Metz, Wulf. 1994. "The Enlightened One: Buddhism." In Eerdmans' Handbook to the World Religions. Pat Alexander, ed. Grand Rapids: Eerdmans.

Moreau, A. Scott. 2000. "Demon, Demonization." In Evangelical Dictionary of World Missions. A. Scott Moreau, Harold Netland, and Charles van Engen, eds. Grand Rapids: Baker.

Overmyer, Daniel. 1993. "Religions of China." In Religious Traditions of the World. H. Byron Earhart, ed. New York: Harper.

Slick, Matthew J. n.d. Gospel of Judas. Retrieved April 26, 2007 from internet: http://www.carm.org/lost/gospel_of_judas.htm.

Stietencron, Heinrich von, and Hans Küng. 2001 "Man and Salvation in Hindu Religions and Religious Practice: Rite, Myth, and Meditation." In Global Civilization, Classical World: Reader, vol 2. William L. Osborne and Ralph D. Winter, eds. Pasadena: William Carey Library.

Yamauchi, Edwin M. 1993. "Gnosis, Gnosticism." In Dictionary of Paul and his Letters, Gerald F. Hawthorne, Ralph P. Martin, and Daniel G. Reid, eds. Downers Grove: InterVarsity.

__________ 1998. "Zoroastrianism." In Global Civilization, Ancient World: Reader, Second Edition, volume 2, eds. William L. Osborne and Ralph D. Winter, Pasadena: William Carey Library,

The Lost Gospel of Judas (n.d.). Retrieved April 26, 2007 from internet: http://www.nationalgeographic.com/lostgospel/about_faq.html.

Wright , N.T. 2006. As One Who Serves. Retrieved April 26, 2007 from internet: http://www.ntwrightpage.com/sermons/As_One_Who_Serves.htm.

Audio Resources, accessed from www.library.wciu.edu/archives

* Create International – Calvin and Carol Conkey

* Foundations of WCIU - Beth Snodderly

* Frickenburg Review – H.L. Richard

* Crisis in Orissa - Vishal Mangalwadi

THE EMBARRASSINGLY DELAYED EDUCATION OF RALPH D. WINTER

Ralph D. Winter

Ralph D. Winter was the founder and former president of William Carey International University. He was serving as Chancellor at the time of his death on May 20, 2009. He is considered by the evangelical world to be one of the foremost missionary statesmen of the 20th century.

Everything here represents either widely accepted scientific understanding or biblical interpretations that are seriously believed by widely respected Bible scholars. Granted that some of these ideas may seem unusual, to my knowledge there is nothing here that can fairly be construed as heresy. Further explanations are at the end.

What About The Gospel?

I could have and would have used the word "Gospel" in what follows were its meaning not highly reduced in common Evangelical usage. In the Bible the word does not refer merely to the heralding of good news but the coming of the Kingdom of God in this world. That is good news. It is also the implantation and extension of God's will in this world. We read more than once in the New Testament about "obeying" or "disobeying the Gospel." Even "hearing" the Gospel implies a yielding to God's will, not just listening and assenting to the truth of a message.

Thus, to "hear" the Gospel means an acceptance of the lordship of Jesus Christ and vital, total involvement in the phrase of the Lord's prayer, "Thy will be done on earth." We see the same thing in the Great Commission's "teaching them to obey all things I have commanded you." All this implies the extension of God's will on earth not just telling people how to get to heaven. Only if believers are known for both seeking and standing up for God's will in all and every part of life can we properly glorify God. Otherwise we misrepresent Him. And, as a result our conversions are half way conversions that may not last or may not truly happen at all.

1950

Soon after 1950, when I was 26 years old, discussions at the level of the Wheaton College Board (following the views of Dr. Russell Mixter, Chair of Wheaton's Dept. of Biological Sciences) came to a significant decision. The board determined that Wheaton faculty would be allowed to believe that the flood in Genesis was local, covering "the known world" but not the entire planet. Of course, once you speculate that Genesis did not necessarily refer to the entire planet, other new interpretations of the first few chapters of Genesis loom. In any case, in 1950 I had no knowledge of this decision at Wheaton. Neither did it occur to me that any Bible believer would take that position. I would not find out about Wheaton's decision until thirty years later.

1958

Eight years after Wheaton's decision, the widely respected department chair of Old Testament Studies at Dallas Theological Seminary, Merrill Unger, went into print (*Bibliotheca Sacra*, 1958) with a highly unconventional view of Genesis 1:1, 2, namely, that Genesis 1:1 was a new beginning, not THE beginning. That is, Genesis chapter 1 is the beginning of *the human story* and not the beginning of *the universe*. But it was not until I was 80, 46 years later, that I typed into Google the words "before Genesis 1:1" and thus learned of Unger's point of view about "the geologic ages" occurring before Genesis 1:1.

1969

Then, it was in 1969, when I was 50, that the USA landed on the Moon. But it would be 28 more years, when I was 78, before I heard that what we found there included the fact that the numerous, quite visible Moon craters (unobliterated by weather or erosion) were actually asteroidal impact craters not volcanic craters—as had long been believed.

2007

Now, in 2007, it has been 32 years since the Moon landing. Ever since then hundreds of scientists have been scouring the surface of our weather-swept earth for similar asteroidal impacts. Hundreds of huge craters have been discovered and thousands of smaller ones. Now, for example, many specialized scientists believe that the 100-million-year dominance of the dinosaurs was suddenly ended by the global turbulence created when a huge asteroid left a 100-mile wide crater in the Yucatan peninsula of Mexico. Indeed, one study reported in *Scientific American* (March 2002) tells of the discovery of 45 impact craters at least 15 miles wide. Furthermore, it is understood that even smaller asteroidal impacts often darken the whole earth until, as the dust settles, first glimmers of light indicating light and day appear and later the Sun, the Moon and stars become visible—a sequence which, if that of Genesis 1, is a sequence of *restoration* not of *creation*.

Something very strange and puzzling but widely discussed by both paleontologists and evolutionists is the sudden and very wide diversity of life forms appearing in what is called the *Cambrian period*. That sudden, spectacular diversity is why this period is usually referred to as the Cambrian *Explosion*. Such an event obviously damages seriously the idea of a gradual Darwinian process. However, where have I been? I did not know until recently that a not-often-mentioned peculiarity of the Cambrian period, in addition to the very-often-mentioned sudden, un-Darwinian profusion of life, was the first appearance at that time of *predatory, life-destroying life*. I first saw this in *National Geographic* and later in technical books on paleontology. Was the Cambrian event the first clear evidence of C. S. Lewis' "Hideous Strength"? More specifically, has the slow progression of increasingly complex life forms been the work of obedient angels—while the violent, predatory life forms have been the effect of angels whose rebellion caused the distortion and violence first appearing in the Cambrian Period? Is that why, when Satan appeared much later in the Garden, he already had a lengthy crime record? Did he "fall" when the Cambrian Period began 500 million years earlier, thus explaining the unremitting destruction, suffering and wildly diverse, violent animal life for the next 500 million years?

Back to Unger. His exegesis of Genesis 1:1, 2 (along with C. I. Scofield and a host of other Bible expositors) proposes that v. 2 describes the result of some sort of a destructive event. *Tohu wa bohu* in v.2 could mean "destroyed and desolate," not merely "formless and void."[1] In that case such a destruction was the basis for the creative events in chapter 1. Furthermore, notice that the text of chapter 1 insists that both the animal and human life created at that time was not predatory or carnivorous. Hmm.

At What Point Humans?

Furthermore, paleohistorians and paleoneurologists may have a better idea of when truly human beings first appeared than ordinary paleontologists whose focus is fossilized bones. Paleoneurologists, in contrast, look to changes in genomics. Paleohistorians pay attention to evidences of unprecedented intelligence rather than to the sizes and shapes of bones. Paleohistorians have come to the fairly settled conclusion that both plants and animals began to be genetically engineered through highly intelligent selective breeding about 11,000 years ago. Recent articles (even Newsweek, Mar 19, 2007) suggest that truly human forms appeared 50,000, or 37,000 or even 5,800 years ago. These are the dates when three unique genes first appeared that are apparently essential to true human beings.

The third of these unique genes, ASPM, clocked in at the 5,800-year date. Could ASPM be the unique "Edenic Gene" characterizing Adam's stock in Eden? If so, this could mean that prior to Eden humans lacking this third gene were living all over the world. Widespread evidences are that such humans were vicious and carnivorous cannibals.[2] Were some of them wiped out in an area of the Middle East when the impact of a smallish asteroid initiated the events of Genesis?

If that happened, the later breakdown of the Edenic new beginning would have resulted in the interbreeding of the animal and human life of Genesis 1 with the already-distorted and carnivorous forms of life outside of the Garden of Eden. This would have caused a degradation of the unique "image of God" type of Edenic humanity (bearing the ASPM gene). That interbreeding would have meant both moral degradation as well as genetic distortion in the form of carnivorous behavior (chapter 9) and the resulting steady shortening of life.

The creation of a "new man" in Christ undoubtedly restores spiritual life that was extinguished by Adam's sin—sin which was guaranteed to cause (and did cause) instant (spiritual) "death." But spiritual restoration would not necessarily roll back genetic distortions, which may be what we call original sin. Are we humans not still carnivorous in our digestive systems? Despite being spiritually transformed by Christ do we not still need both our shotguns and immune systems as long as both large animals and microscopic forms of life are still dangerous? Does not, as in Romans 7, our spiritual nature still fight against our physical nature? The "renewing of our minds" in Romans 12:1 curbs our inherited bestiality except when we may run berserk like Hutu pastors wielding machetes in Rwanda. The "old man" is still there unless crucified daily.

Thus?

If this scenario is by any chance correct, then there is clearly no contradiction between the Bible and the latest thinking of contemporary paleontology and paleoneurology. There is no conflict if the universe is 13.7 billion years old. There is no problem if the Earth is 4.5 billion years old. The simplest forms of life may very well have begun to appear 4 billion years ago.

Then, after 3.5 billion years of the intensive labors of angels who were all good (and, under God's guidance, tinkering with DNA) life forms would develop to a threshold where already larger animals (not vicious nor predatory) would finally appear.

At that point, totally unexpectedly, after 3.5 billion years of development, during just the next, most recent, half-billion years (one eighth of the time), massive distortion, chaos, suffering and pain would suddenly appear as good angels continuously fought rebel angels led by Satan. During these last 500 million years life would continue to get more and more complex and fabulously diverse, as teams of good angels developed new and creative life forms in different parts of the world, but now having to arm them with defensive traits in all-out war against the constant counter distortions of evil angels.

This lengthy, contested development of life forms, contrary to Darwinian Evolution, could have been a process similar to that of thousands of intelligent engineers across the 20th century developing different but similar automobiles in different parts of the world with ever increasing complexity. Unlike unguided Darwinian processes, however, is the fact that no manufacturer developed cars that ate other cars! By contrast, all life forms are subject to premature death and destruction. And, in such a scenario (of good angels developing new and more sophisticated forms of life), it would not seem strange—it would be expected—that new models would be closely similar to earlier forms of life. That is, finding "missing links" would not prove *unguided evolution* any more than it would confirm *continuity of intelligent design.*

Curiously, ever since the Cambrian Period 500 million years ago, asteroidal collisions have apparently repeatedly knocked out much of life on earth, the dinosaurs being one of the most curious and violent species to perish suddenly. Perhaps they deserved destruction? In this scenario, the destruction of all life in even a local area would have produced initial global darkness and then the restorative sequence described in Genesis chapter 1. All this could have been witnessed and remembered by intelligent (but distorted, bestial and predatory) human beings outside of the area of Eden. The breakdown of the Garden of Eden would have then exposed both animal and human life (created, as in Genesis 1:29-30, in a non-carnivorous state) to forms of life that were distinctly carnivorous and violent, and the "fall" of man would then ensue.

This would then mean that Adam's "fall" would have brought a curse upon Edenic life and initiated globally a struggle against the corruption and evil of Satan's doing, good angels working together with reconciled man in a struggle against darkness. This is essentially the story of the Bible as well as the last two millennia.

> Mission and evangelism then can be seen as a means of recruiting and renewing humans in a struggle which is not basically between God and man but between God-plus-redeemed-man against the kingdom of Satan and his works.

This is a battle to restore in people's minds the glory of God by helping people to see that not only human but angelic *evil is to be identified with Satanic initiative and not God's initiative*—a fact widely and extensively misunderstood in Evangelical circles today, witness James Dobson's earnest but misleading book, *When God Doesn't Make Sense*. Or, witness a Harvard professor's unchallengeable statement: "If the God of Intelligent Design exists he must be a divine sadist who creates parasites that blind millions of people." Or witness the testimony of a world famous professor of Biblical studies, a Moody Bible Institute and Wheaton graduate, the prolific, erudite professor at Duke, Bart Ehrman,

> This made me think more deeply about my own understanding of why there is suffering in the world. Finally, because I became dissatisfied with all of the conventional answers I decided that I could not believe in [a] God who was in any way intervening in this world given the state of things. So that's how I ended up losing my faith.

In order to glorify God we must resist the common idea that all events are initiated by God. We are to rejoice in and praise God *in all things* but not rejoice and praise God *for all things*. As long as angels and men have free will God is not in the usual sense the initiator of all things.

This scenario is the very opposite of sitting back and assuming that God does all things both good and bad. Rather, it explains the urgent and momentous obligation to distinguish evil from good and to fight all evil and every evil with everything in our command (not just first century knowledge).

The scope of the Christian mission that then devolves on every follower of Christ is to seek constantly what is the maximum contribution he or she can make to glorifying God and fighting evil. This includes healing the sick, rescuing those who are suffering for any reason, preventing disease and malice, and eliminating or eradicating sources of evil and disease. It requires us to engage meaningfully in the global battle against human slavery, corruption in both government and private enterprise, family breakdown, and so forth.

In most cases it is necessary to *organize*. It is not enough for individual believers to do good deeds. Individuals can do much but many things require group action. In some cases groups, such as mission agencies, already exist. In many cases new organizations need to be initiated. It is not necessary to fly a church or even a "Jesus" flag. In the long run God will get the glory. Otherwise what we do may be interpreted as a means of aggrandizing our particular faith. ***But clearly, fighting evil is instant common ground with every group and society. Winning people over to our religious/cultural tradition is not.***

Afterview

Is Christian faith blossoming around the world today only to fade tomorrow when it faces the hard questions of today's anti-religious onslaught?

The exploding power of both Muslim fundamentalists and the Evangelical movement has elicited an almost equally powerful backlash against religion in general, and against those who are *sincerely* religious in particular. It is the *sincere* who are considered the most dangerous! They are the ones who blow themselves up or shoot abortion doctors!

The anti-religious backlash is intelligent, widespread, and desperate, fully confident of its cause. Science is more trustworthy than religious dogma. Young people by the thousands, even those from devout homes, are being carried away by assaults on both the Bible and the Christian historical record.

Probably the most vexing and ineffective Christian teaching is what we come up with in the face of tragic and evil events. Why does God allow such things? One young person after his freshman year at college said to his Dad "There is so much evil, suffering, and injustice in the world that either there is no God at all or there is a God of questionable power or character." This idea is all the more devastating when Evangelicals, having essentially given up believing in an intelligent Enemy of God, take to explaining tediously that all this evil must be because God's ways are simply mysterious. Satan, rampant and powerful in the New Testament, has mainly disappeared from significance following Augustine's injection of some neo-platonic thought into the Christian tradition.

Even more common, if possible, and equally destructive, is the common saying that the Bible is clearly of no value as long as it baldly proposes that the universe is only 6,000 years old.

In other words, here are two significant barriers to Christian belief: the rampant evil in this world if there is no Satan behind it, and a Bible with the feet of clay if Genesis 1:1 is thought to be the beginning of everything 6000 years ago.

Both of these obstacles to belief can be dealt with in an unusual way.

Thus, what was first described in this chapter is a brief scenario that attempts conjecturally to interpret Genesis in such a way as not to conflict with the very latest scientific views. This approach may be helpful in dealing with either non-Christians or Christians about to lose their faith. It may also be helpful to people who believe current science is mainly correct in regard to 1) how old the earth is, and, 2) how long ago humans first appeared, but for whom the two things discussed above are difficult to square with the Bible.

Elsewhere I have written about a view that differs from the view of many scientists in that it explains the development of life by a means quite different from a Darwinian style random process. Furthermore, it allows for much of both the so-called "Young Earth" and the "Old Earth" perspectives. Most of all, it highlights a striking new dimension in the definition of Christian mission. The key stages in the story derive from my own growing up experience.

Editor's Note: *For an overview of this perspective, see the next chapter, "The Warfare Worldview of Ralph D. Winter."*

End Notes

1. Old Testament scholars translate *tohu wabohu* with such terms as "desolation and disorder" (John Gibson, *Daily Study Bible Series: Genesis*, Vol. 1. Louisville, Kentucky: Westminster, John Knox Press, 1981,), "welter and waste" (Robert Alter, *The Five Books of Moses: A Translation with Commentary*. New York: W. W. Norton & Co., p. ix), "chaos and desolation" (Bernhard Anderson, *From Creation to New Creation: OT Perspectives*. Minneapolis: Fortress, p. 11).

2. *"Clear evidence of cannibalism in the human fossil record has been [considered] rare, but it is now becoming apparent that the practice is deeply rooted in our history."* (Tim D. White. "Once Were Cannibals." *Scientific American, August 2001, Vol. 285 Issue 2: 58.)*

References

Alvarez, Walter. *T.* 1997. Rex & the Crater of Doom. Princeton: Princeton Univ. Press.

Becker, Luann. 2002. "Repeated Blows." *Scientific American*, March: 76-83.

Dobson, James. 1997. When God Doesn't Make Sense. Wheaton: Tyndale House.

Eldredge, John. 2004. The Epic. Nashville: Thomas Nelson.

Fortey, Richard. 1998. *Life: A Natural History of the 1st 4 billion Years of Life on Earth.* (New York: Alfred A. Knopf, p. 82, 92-93).

Pinker, Steven. 2005. Quoted in David Van Biema. "Can You Believe in God and Evolution?" *Time*, August 7.

Unger, Merrill F. 1958 "Rethinking the Genesis Account of Creation." *Bibliotheca Sacra* 115: 27-35.

White, Tim D. 2001. "Once Were Cannibals." *Scientific American,* 285: 58.

Zeder, Melinda A. and Brian Hesse. 2000. "The Initial Domestication of Goats (Capra hircus) in the Zagros Mountains 10,000 Years Ago." *Science* (24 March).

THE WARFARE WORLDVIEW OF RALPH D. WINTER

Beth Snodderly

This article was written while the author was doing doctoral research with Ralph Winter as the major advisor. It attempts to provide biblical and scientific evidence for several of his controversial proposals and speculations.

Five premises are highlighted in this chapter that reflect the worldview behind Ralph Winter's thinking:

1. God is the Lord of history, but we are locked in a cosmic struggle.

2. God reveals himself, but an intelligent evil power distorts both general and special revelation and all of God's handiwork. God did not create or intend evil, but He created spirit and human beings with free will who chose to use their free will to rebel against Him.

3. God desires humans to work with Him as agents in history for His purposes in defeating evil.

4. On the basis of Jesus' life, death, and resurrection, God defeats evil and redeems and restores humanity and creation.

5. The widely acknowledged evidence regarding the age of the earth and development of life, from paleontology, geology and other sciences, can be taken seriously for the purposes of this paper.

Distortions of God's Good Purposes

Something is wrong in this world. "Nature, red in tooth and claw," is a pattern acted out at all levels of life, from micropredators (disease caused by microbes) to macropredators (social diseases caused by humans such as war and slavery). Intelligent evil is at work in this world, distorting God's original good purposes.

Distortions of human social relations, distortions of nature ("natural disasters"), distortions by disease: all these are the categories represented by three of the horses of the apocalypse (war, famine, and plague), all leading to death (Rev. 6: 3-8). In addition, the description of the last ("pale") horse includes death by wild animals, which was not in God's original plan (Genesis 1:30). It is also excluded from His final plan when wolves will lie down with the lambs, lions will eat straw like an ox, and children will play near snakes without being harmed (Isaiah 11:6-9).

If God is all-powerful and all-loving, and has such wonderful plans for the planet's future, why does He permit the obvious evil we see now in nature and in "man's inhumanity to man"?

Why has God allowed sadistic people throughout history to torture others in unimaginably horrible ways?

Is God pleased when a tsunami wipes out hundreds of thousands of people without warning?

Is God glorified by what greatly troubled Darwin, that a particular kind of wasp lays its eggs inside a caterpillar so that when the eggs hatch, the larvae eat their way out of the caterpillar while it is still living?

Do diseases such as cancer, AIDS, malaria, and small pox, that literally eat people alive, originate from organisms designed by a perfect and good Creator?

What went wrong?

"The creation waits in eager expectation for the sons of God to be revealed. ... We know that the whole creation has been groaning as in the pains of childbirth right up to the present time" (Romans 8:20-22).

Origins of Evil

Ralph Winter has proposed a story about the origins of evil on this planet, developed and documented briefly here. (See the End Notes for more detail.) This story firmly attributes the source of this evil to spirit beings (Satan in particular and his many demonic followers), who chose to use their God-given gift of free will to rebel against God. [1]

The story places responsibility for overcoming that evil on the shoulders of humans—specifically those who are followers of Christ—who were created in the expectation that they would choose to use their gift of free will to say, "thy Kingdom come, thy will be done" and to participate with God in defeating the evil one and restoring creation to its intended state of displaying the glory of God.

Under a burden of evil that God did not intend for it, creation groans as it waits for the Body of Christ to fulfill its purpose to work with God to defeat evil and its resulting distortions. David Neff commented recently in *Christianity Today*, "as Christians we cannot be honest about reality without seeing the world as a struggle between good and evil" (2005: 76). The free will of humankind aligning itself with God's will is apparently God's plan for overcoming the evil results of choices made by free spirit beings. [2]

The Story Begins

"In the beginning God created the heavens and the earth" (Genesis 1:1).

The biblical account of creation needs to be considered within its original setting. In the Near Eastern world at the time Genesis was written, creation stories were full of titanic struggles between good and evil spiritual forces that preceded the creation of the world and of humans. We can assume that the people God chose to work through already knew of these myths and of the existence of good and evil spirits. [3] The difference in the biblical account from these surrealistic myths is the perspective that at the beginning of time a good God intelligently created a good world.

Recent scientific thinking has led to the "Big Bang" theory of the origin of the universe. According to this modern scientific creation myth, as historian David Christian calls it, "thirteen billion years ago there was nothing. There wasn't even emptiness. Time did not exist, nor did space. In this nothing, there occurred an explosion, and within a split second, something did exist" (2004: 497). Well-known physicist Stephen Hawking states, "almost everyone now believes that the universe, and time itself, had a beginning at the big bang" (Hawking and Penrose, 1995: 20). Through forces of extreme heat and gravity, gradually the simplest atoms of helium and hydrogen fused in a variety of combinations and other elements and objects came into existence.

Development of Life

 From this scientific perspective, life began relatively late in the timeline and evolved gradually. In this slow development, the first life forms were anaerobic and lived in the ocean. Scientist Andrew Parker speculates that the earth may have been going through a galactic dust cloud that blocked sunlight from the earth, making life requiring oxygen impossible for millions of years (2003: 292-294). Comets and meteorites from outer space would have brought some of the organic and trace elements needed for life to begin and develop on this planet (Fortey 1998: 49).

Ralph Winter speculates that life forms were being created by spirit beings whom God was instructing, who were learning to think God's thoughts after Him. In this he echoes J. R. R. Tolkien's account of the creation of earth in *The Silmarillion* in which the music of the "Ainur" reflects what they are learning of the thoughts of "Iluvatar" and eventually they bring these thoughts into reality (1977: 3-12).

Might these speculations have their roots in primordial reality? Is it possible that God's servants worked with Him in Creation, learning how to sculpt the raw materials of the universe into living creatures? Strange, weird life forms and the slow development of life (according to the "record of the rocks") all lend credibility to the speculation that perhaps God deliberately chose not to use His omniscience and omnipotence to create all life forms instantly, but instead shared creation with beings who were learning as they went along.

Free Will

From a theological point of view, God created spiritual beings with free will with the object of receiving their freely chosen love. But this entailed a risk. With the power to choose, there could be no guarantee that the free beings would make choices that would also be God's choices. (Boyd 1997:19)

G.K. Chesterton suggests God was writing a play:

> God had written, not so much a poem, but rather a play; a play he had planned as perfect, but which had necessarily been left to human actors and stage-managers, [and other beings with free will], who had since made a great mess of it (Chesterton 1908).

Within the parameters of the guidelines for this "play," it seems that God has placed some limitations on himself according to what free agents freely choose. Boyd states, "Unless we affirm that God takes genuine risks, we will not be able to acknowledge that the world is a war zone while also holding that this war is not God's will" (2001: 86).

Cambrian Explosion: The Fall of Satan?

Continuing with the scientific creation "myth," at a particular point in time, according to the evidence from the fossil record, there was a sudden proliferation of life on this planet: complete with predators and defense mechanisms (Fortey 1998: 92, 93; Parker 2003: 259).

Parker states that an external force has to be taken into account to explain the Cambrian explosion, in which there was the sudden development (in the "blink of an eye" in geological terms) of hard body parts in all biological categories of life (2003: 36). Parker's research led him to the conclusion that it was the sudden appearance of vision in one evolving creature at the beginning of the Cambrian period that led to selective pressures for all the various phyla to also develop eyes, then hard parts to stab with, "limbs to perform their acts of murder" (because they saw potential food and wanted it!), and hard body parts for defense mechanisms (Parker 2003: 276).

But what caused the sudden development of eyes and the simultaneous onset of violence in 35 phyla, all within a relatively short period of time? The scientific creation myth claims it was evolutionary chance along with selective evolutionary pressures.

Ralph Winter asks, regarding the sudden appearance of violent forms of life, could this be when the fall of Satan occurred?

Going still further, we could speculate that Lucifer, whose name means "morning star, light-bearing" (Webster's Third New International Dictionary), may have been responsible for the development of eyesight, that he became proud of his accomplishment, rebelled against God (in Luke 10:18 Jesus says, "I saw Satan fall like lightning from heaven"), and began turning his creative knowledge into distortions of God's creation.

The early Church Fathers believed a story very similar to the one described by Ralph Winter: the participation of angels in creation, Satan's original place of authority, territorial responsibilities of angels and evil spirits, and the entrance of evil into creation with the choices made by Satan/Lucifer and his followers (Boyd 2001: 294, 295).

Alvin Plantinga, considered the "dean" of Christian philosophers (Beverley 2005: 83), writes in a chapter in *Christian Faith and the Problem of Evil*,

> Satan is a mighty non-human free creature who rebelled
> against the Lord long before human beings were on the scene;
> and much of the natural evil the world displays is due to the
> actions of Satan and his cohorts. (Van Inwagen 2004: 15)

The Reality of the Spirit World

This perspective on the reality of the world of spirits sounds foreign to western thinkers and believers because of the philosophical influence of the Enlightenment that insists that all reality must follow observable laws. But this relatively brief 300-year materialist worldview is in the minority within the context of past and non-western worldviews. In a key article in the *Perspectives on the World Christian Movement* Reader, Paul Hiebert points out the "flaw of the excluded middle" (referring to the spirit realm) in western thinking (1999: 414).

Harmonizing Science and Scripture

Given the reality of an active spirit world, Ralph Winter's speculative story harmonizes scientific evidence and biblical teaching. To summarize the argument constructed up to this point, we can look at Winter's paper in IJFM 21:4 that lists his personal "Precarious Perspectives" (2005a: 53), the first three of which state:

> #1. Evidence is mounting that life has been developing on this planet over a very long time.
> #2. Suddenly in the Cambrian Period we find in the world of animals the first appearance of predatory life forms.
> #3. Nature has been pervasively distorted into violence by Satan.

The third "Perspective" goes on to state that "these violent forms of life are again and again blotted out by devastations" (2005a: 53).

Expanding a chart from *Scientific American*, March 2002, Winter has described a 600 million year timeline that includes 45 major asteroidal impacts that would have destroyed much of life on this planet at many different times in history. One of the two largest of these, causing a 100-mile-wide crater in Yucatan, Mexico, is believed to have caused the extinction of the dinosaurs 60 million years ago. After that a new beginning featured large mammals and hominids (pre-human creatures) as dominant life forms on the planet (Winter 2005a: 51).

Winter's expanded chart postulates a local asteroidal devastation in the Near East prior to 6000 BC. The literary, realistic description in Genesis 1:2-19 fits very well with Winter's hypothesis that the biblical writer was describing the "re-creation" of a local area from the perspective of an observer on earth watching the gradual settling of dust, making light visible once again, making plant life possible, then eventually making it possible for the individual heavenly bodies that are the source of the light to become visible, as night and day are clearly distinguished. [1]

Winter and others such as Bruce K. Waltke (2001) believe it may be a disservice to the Bible to interpret the Genesis Creation account as the beginning of everything, but rather see it as the record of a new beginning following the devastation referred to in Genesis 1:2 as "tohu wabohu."

Winter's "Precarious Perspectives" #7 and #8 summarize this thinking:

> #7. The idea that the "old earth" preceded the "young earth" and preceded Genesis 1:1.
>
> #8. The events of Genesis, the asteroidal devastation described in 1:1, and the flood mentioned later, are devastations and new beginnings, re-creation, replenishment (Winter 2005a: 53).

In his presumption that the Genesis creation account describes a re-creation of the world, Winter agrees with Eric Sauer, quoted by Boyd:

> Genesis 1 is not so much an account of creation as it is an account of God's restoration of a world that had through a previous conflict become formless, futile, empty and engulfed by chaos—the world of Gen 1:2 (1997:104).

A comprehensive study shows that the context Hebrew words for "formless" and "empty"("*tohu wabohu*") refers to the chaos resulting from God's judgment on societies in rebellion against His ways.

War against an Intelligent Enemy

This battlefield is the warfare context in which humans were created. We are in a war against an intelligent enemy. "Humans are made in the image of God and placed on earth so that they might gradually vanquish this chaos" (Boyd 1997: 107)), not just to "take care of it" as the cultural mandate describes it. Humans were created to join a war that was already taking place. Winter suggests that the cultural and evangelistic mandates need to be merged into a single "Military Mandate, which in this life is all we should be concerned about" (2005a: 46).

This interpretation of Genesis 1 implies that God's plan to strike back at the enemy was to overcome the free choices of evil agents with the free choices of good agents. Perhaps in God's free will universe He needed more creatures to choose His way, to ask Him to act and to take action to annihilate Evil. If Evil is of finite amount, if it can be "overcome" (annihilated) by freely chosen acts of love and self-sacrifice, then eventually some specific act of love or sacrifice could be expected to annihilate the bit of evil that represents the tipping point, putting the majority of free choices in this world on the side of God's will, thus clearing the way for Him to usher in His Kingdom. Was Jesus' sacrificial death that "tipping point"? Is God waiting for the time when He has enough of the free choices of humans and spirit beings on His side to win the battle at the end of the age, as described in the last book of the Bible?

But at the beginning of human history, humans chose to join the fallen spirit beings in rebellion against God and eventually things got so bad that demons were polluting the human gene pool (Genesis 6; see Boyd 2001:166). The Flood that followed was one of several fresh starts in God's war with evil (Winter 2005a: 51).

Ralph Winter's speculation that evil spirits have tampered with DNA to distort God's intentions for animals or to create organisms whose sole purpose is to cause disease, has biblical support in this Genesis 6 account of the "sons of God" having children with the daughters of men. Could this be a mythological or pre-scientific recognition of the spirit world tampering with the DNA of humans? Is similar tampering the cause of violence in the animal world? Ralph Winter speculates on these questions:

> Humans have concluded that cock fights and contrived animal-versus-animal shows are illegal. ... How much less likely should we suppose God to have created the nearly universal, vicious, animal-versus-animal world of nature? Indeed, carnivorous animals originally were herbivorous (as is implied in Genesis 1:28, 29). Does the Evil One and his assistants have sufficient knowledge to tinker with the DNA of God's created order and distort nature to become "red in tooth and claw"? (2005a: 38).

Obstacles to Opposing Evil

Such evidences of evil are the result of God's decision to give free choice to His servants, both spirit beings and humans. But the evidences of evil are not God's will, although they are often mistakenly attributed to Him. Winter has stated: "If believers have all kinds of misunderstandings that prevent them from 'destroying the works of the Devil' I want desperately to help remove those misunderstandings" (2004).

Several obstacles keep Western believers from recognizing the need to oppose evil in its many forms. One of these obstacles is the failure to recognize the reality of the spirit world and the evil intentions of some of those spirits to distort the physical world. Boyd, Hiebert and others have explained that Western thought about the non-existence of the spirit world, the legacy of the Enlightenment, is in the minority and stands in contrast to the rest of the world throughout history.

Another obstacle to opposing evil is the confusion caused by Augustinian thinking which assumed God's omnipotence meant God was in direct control of everything and had His purposes in permitting evil. In *City of God*, Augustine argued that God permits evil so we will desire the future "blessed life."

> Even baptized infants, who are certainly unsurpassed in innocence, are sometimes so tormented, that God, who permits it, teaches us hereby to bewail the calamities of this life, and to desire the felicity of the life to come. *City of God* 22.22 (Geisler 1982: 192).

The concept of fighting back against atrocities, such as the torment experienced by innocent babies, is missing in Augustine's theology. A logical consequence of his "blueprint" worldview, as Boyd calls it (2001:2), is passivity. If God has pre-ordained all evil for some mysterious purpose, why pray, why act? Why not sadly wait it out until one is able to enter the happier life to come?

In contrast, the authors of the New Testament and the Early Church fathers prior to Augustine expected evil and were prepared to fight it. They had no problem with the concept that a good God had allowed freedom of choice and was bound by His own decision to fight a real war against evil that Christ's followers must join (Boyd 2001: 24, 49).

The Kingdom Strikes Back

The biblical record sets the direction for believers to follow in the fight against evil. Winter's article in the *Perspectives* Reader, "The Kingdom Strikes Back," describes the history of the battle against the evil intelligence that is distorting our world.

> The Bible shows the gradual but irresistible power of God reconquering and redeeming His fallen creation; giving His own Son at the center of the 4000 year period beginning with 2000 BC. ...'The Son of God appeared for this purpose, that He might destroy the works of the devil' (1 John 3:8) (Winter 1999: 196).

Jesus' Acts of War against Evil

From the very first, Jesus' acts of ministry made it clear that He had come to wage war against evil. His encounters with demons always resulted in glory for God. Even the evil influences on nature had to obey Him when He rebuked the storm (Mark 4: 39) with the same authority He used in casting out evil spirits (Mark 5:8). "If it is by the finger of God that I cast out the demons," Jesus said, "then the kingdom of God has come to you" (Luke 11:20).

Jesus' death is seen as the climax of a cosmic battle in an exposition of John 12: 20-36 (Kovac 1995: 233). "Now shall the ruler of this world be driven out," (vs. 31) Jesus said, in the context of discussing His death.

Jesus passed His mission on to His followers, teaching them to pray that God's will would be done "on earth as it is in heaven" (Matthew 6:10) and telling them the gates of hell would not prevail against the Church's initiatives. Jesus did what He saw the Father doing (John 5:19) and He told His followers they would do even greater things than He had been doing (John 14:12).

Believers' Acts of War against Evil

In His decision to work through the Body of Christ to expand Jesus' ministry of pushing back the powers of darkness, God has chosen to use the foolish and weak things of the world to overthrow the wise and strong in the world who resist Him (1 Corinthians 1:18-30). Romans 12 and 1 Corinthians 12 give brief theologies of the Body of Christ. When Christ's Body, the Church, is functioning as it should, it demonstrates the nature of God: what works He wants to see accomplished, what He is concerned about, His righteousness, justice, mercy, and power over evil. Since the Son of God appeared to destroy the devil's work (1 John 3:8), this is also the mission of His Body. In the article, "The Kingdom Strikes Back," Ralph Winter describes five epochs of church history in which, almost in spite of the behavior of many representatives of the Church, the Kingdom has gradually advanced around the world (1999: 195).

This advance is occurring even in the context of the weeds and the good seed growing side by side. The two conflicting kingdoms will each continue to grow until Christ returns. (This perspective is a distinctive of Eastern Orthodox theology [Campolo 1992: 45]).

Winter 's "Precarious Perspective #4" describes what it means for the Kingdom to advance.

> Evangelicals rightly stress a reconciliation-of-man aspect and a promise of heaven. ... But, in addition, they have not emphasized, as clearly as the Bible does, God's glorification (that is, the re-establishment, the restoration of that glory) (2005a: 49).

What is the believer's responsibility in restoring God's glory and advancing the Kingdom?

Prayer and Action

Prayer and action need to go together in defeating evil and restoring God's glory. Winter likes to point out that we don't ask God to paint the back fence; we get out there and do it ourselves. Another Winter illustration: If you saw a mountain lion attacking a child, you wouldn't stop to pray, you'd do something about it (just as Donald McGavran used to shoot tigers to protect villagers in India). But if "invisible lions" (i.e. germs) were attacking a child, you would appropriately ask for God's intervention (2005d).

A general principle might be: evils you can see, take action; with evils you can't see, ask God to take action. Until recently in history, people couldn't see the micro-organisms ("invisible lions") attacking people, animals and crops. Now that science has made it possible to see and do something about these micro-predators, what is the responsibility of the Body of Christ?

Newbigin quotes Schweitzer as saying, "Every action for the Kingdom is a prayer for the coming of the Kingdom" (Newbigin 2003: 38). Boyd points out that Water Wink and others have shown that combating evil powers is not just a matter of prayer but also a matter of social activism (Boyd 1997:60). Winter would add, "and of scientific activism."

In fact, prayer itself may be activism. Jesus said what is loosed on earth will be loosed in heaven (Matthew 16:19). Could it be that God's self-limited ability to act on earth will be loosed to some extent when a free agent chooses to ask Him and chooses to work with Him to accomplish His purposes?

Overthrowing the Kingdom of Disease and Death

Knowing that wars and diseases of social, "natural" and physical varieties, and the resulting suffering, are not God's will, and that God will some day bring an end to these things (Rev. 20:4) gives the Body of Christ some strong hints about the work they should be engaged in.

Medical missionary Robert Hughes, in Shillong, India from 1939-69, wrote in his journal, "this kingdom of disease, death, ignorance, prejudice, fear, malnutrition and abject poverty was most surely a kingdom which ought to be overthrown by the kingdom of our God" (Rees 2003).

Overthrowing the kingdom of disease and death means engaging in Kingdom warfare. Fighting disease is an integral part of that warfare. The similarities between war and disease are brought out in two books written about disease. The author of *At War Within* uses war imagery to describe diseases of the immune system. For instance, in the preliminary phase of AIDS, "the virus is doing everything it can to break loose from the lymph node environment where it is trapped and to destroy the host, but it is kept in check by the immune system" (Clark 1995: 151). In *Plagues and Peoples*, William McNeill coins the term, "macroparasitism," using disease imagery to describe warlike raiding and other social predatory behavior.

Disease and war are keeping whole groups of people in bondage to suffering and evil. Maps from MARC publications (Myers 1996) and from internet sources show the non-coincidental overlap of areas of the world that have the least influence from the Bible with those areas where there is the most suffering, disease, war and poverty. Barrett and Johnson have shown in a chart in *World Christian Trends* that the "absolute poor" comprise 18% of the world's population while "The Rich" make up 54% of the world (2001: 34). The MARC maps show that main consumers of the earth's natural resources live in those areas of the world with the most exposure to the Bible.

What responsibility does the kingdom believer have for using those resources, in the light of the distribution of evil and God's plan to defeat it? In his address to a large gathering of Korean young people at a missions conference, Winter challenged them on this very issue.

> Every believer has a missionary call. Second Corinthians 5:15 says, 'He died for all, that those who live should *no longer* live for themselves but for him who died for them and was raised again.' Let Jesus take over your life and be concerned about His concerns. What is it He's wanting to do? Disease is pulling people down all the time, distorting human and animal life. Disease is a work of Satan, which the Son of God came to destroy (Winter 2005b).

"Mission" is something all God's people participate in—not just cross-cultural workers. Our mission is to defeat evil and restore God's glory. The business of life is to participate meaningfully in this mission and to pray by our actions, "Your Kingdom come Your will be done on earth as it is in heaven" (Matthew 6:10).

End Notes

1. The literary structure of the Genesis Creation account is seen in the parallelism between the first and second sets of three creation "days."

Day 1: Light

Day 2: Air and water separated

Day 3: Dry land separated from water; vegetation appears

- - - -

Day 4: Specific lights in the sky become visible

Day 5: Creatures begin to live in the air and water

Day 6: Creatures begin to live on dry land: animals, humans created and given green plants to eat.

References

Barrett, David and Todd Johnson. 2001. World Christian Trends. Pasadena: William Carey Library.

Boyd, Gregory A. 1997. God at War: The Bible and Spiritual Conflict. Downer's Grove: InterVarsity Press.

__________. 2001. Satan and the Problem of Evil. Downers Grove: InterVarsity Press.

Campolo, Tony. 1992. How to Rescue the Earth without Worshiping Nature: A Christian's Call to Save Creation. Nashville: Thomas Nelson.

Cartwright, Frederick in collaboration with Michael D. Biddiss. 1972. Disease in History. New York: Barnes & Noble Books.

Clark, William R. 1995. At War Within: The Double-Edged Sword of Immunity. New York: Oxford University Press.

Chesterton, G.K. 1908. Orthodoxy. Internet: Christian Classics Ethereal Library. (Chapter 5: Optimism and Pessimism.)

Christian, David. 2004. Maps of Time: An Introduction to Big History.

Dom Bruno Well. 1941. Why Does God Permit Evil? London: Burns, Oates, and Washbourne Ltd.

Fortey, Richard A. 1998. Life: a Natural History of the First Four Billion Years of Life on Earth. New York: Alfred A. Knopf.

Geisler, Norman L., Editor. 1982. What Augustine Says. Grand Rapids: Baker.

Hawking, Stephen and Roger Penrose. 1996. The Nature of Space and Time. Princeton: Princeton University Press.

Hiebert, Paul. 1999. Flaw of the Excluded Middle. *In* Perspectives on the World Christian Movement, 3rd edition, ed. Ralph D. Winter and Steven C. Hawthorne, editors. Pages 414-419. Pasadena: William Carey Library.

Kovac, J.L. 1995. Now Shall the Ruler of This World Be Driven Out: Death as Cosmic Battle in John 12:20-36, Journal of Biblical Literature 114:233.

Lewis, C. S. 1940. The Problem of Pain. London: Geoffrey Bles.

McNeill, William H. 1976. Plagues and Peoples. New York: Anchor Press/Doubleday.

Myers, Bryant L. 1996. The New Context of World Mission. Monrovia, CA: MARC.

Newbigin, Lesslie. 2003. Signs amid the Rubble: The Purposes of God in Human History. Ed. Geoffrey Wainwright. Grand Rapids: Eerdmans.

Parker, Andrew. 2003. In the Blink of an Eye. Cambridge, MA: Perseus Publications.

Rees, D. Ben, ed. 2003. Vehicles of Grace and Hope: Welsh Missionaries in India 1800 - 1970. Pasadena: William Carey Library.

Sider, Ron. 2005. The Evangelical Scandal. Christianity Today, pp. 70-73. April.

Tolkien, J.R.R. 1977. The Silmarillion. New York: Ballantine Books.

Van Inwagen, Peter, Editor. 2004.Christian Faith and the Problem of Evil. Grand Rapids: Eerdmans.

Waltke, Bruce K. with Cathi J. Fredricks. 2001. Genesis: A Commentary. Grand Rapids: Zondervan.

Winter, Ralph W. 1999. The Kingdom Strikes Back. *In* Perspectives on the World Christian Movement, 3rd edition, ed. Ralph D. Winter and Steven C. Hawthorne, editors. Pages 195-213. Pasadena: William Carey Library.

________. 2004. Disease/evil explanations. Email to snoke@pitt.edu. July 8.

________. 2005a. Frontiers in Mission: Discovering and Surmounting Barriers to the Missio Dei. Pasadena: WCIU Press.

________. 2005b. The Missio Dei. Plenary Address to One in Love (OIL) Conference, Philadelphia. January.

________. 2005c Evil/Augustine. Author's interview with Ralph Winter, February 18.

________. 2005d.   Business and Mission. Author's interview with Ralph Winter, March 11.

________. 2005e. A New Frontier: Business as Mission. Non-published article. March 26.

Yamamori, Tetsunao and Kim-Kwong Chan. 2002. Holistic Entrepreneurs in China: A Handbook on the World Trade Organization and New Opportunities for Christians. Pasadena: WCIU Press.

Yamamori, Tetsunao and Kenneth A. Eldred, Editors. 2003. On Kingdom Business: Transforming Missions through Entrepreneurial Strategies. Wheaton: Crossway Books.

GENESIS 6 AND RALPH WINTER'S THEORY OF ANGELIC CORRUPTION OF CREATION

David Taylor

David Taylor is a graduate student with William Carey International University and is a guest editor and contributor to the journal, Mission Frontiers. He has served as assistant to the chair of the program committee for the world level Tokyo 2010 gathering.

The late Dr. Ralph Winter proposed the possibility that fallen angels were involved in the corruption of creation as we find it today. This paper, while not attempting to prove this supposition, will endeavor to make a small contribution to this concept by unearthing a significant article of biblical evidence that may lend credibility to Winter's theory. This key piece of evidence can be found in the Flood account of Genesis 6 relating to a group of beings referred to as the *Nephilim*, which literally means "the fallen ones." (Wiersbe 2007, 36)[1] Although variously interpreted, this paper will seek to demonstrate why an "angelic" interpretation of this passage has the greatest merit and why it holds significant value for Dr. Ralph Winter's theory.

Introducing Ralph Winter's Theory

In a paper entitled, "The Story of Our Planet," Winter proposed that the "mystery of predatory life" could be explained by the possibility that Satan treacherously interfered with God's purposes for life on earth. Winter postulated:

> If God had been employing thousands of intelligent, angelic beings in the process of elaborating and developing life, and if one

of the chief leaders of those intelligent beings were to have turned against Him, would that not explain the sudden presence of life-destroying forms of life in the Cambrian period?...

Thus, a better explanation for the massive suffering and premature death in nature might be . . . the possibility that many forms of life at all levels of size and complexity, although earlier created benign, have been distorted into vicious mutations by a skillful, destructive tampering with their DNA by the Evil One and his evil servants (whether human or angelic). (2005, 254-55)

It is important to note that Winter was not saying that angels had "creative" power in the sense of being able to bring something into existence *ex nihilo*. But what he was arguing was that just as humans have the ability to tinker with DNA, so do angelic beings. His purpose in making this claim was to give a rationale for why redeemed humans should be involved in reversing the damage caused by these fallen angels, as well as restoring glory to God by removing from Him any blame that might be attributed to Him for the corruption we find in nature.

Interpreting Genesis 6

A critical piece of evidence supporting Dr. Winter's theory that angels can manipulate our "material" world may be found in the Genesis Flood passage, specifically in verses 1-4 of chapter 6:

When men began to increase in number on the earth and daughters were born to them, the sons of God saw that the daughters of men were beautiful, and they married any of them they chose. Then the Lord said, "My Spirit will not contend with man forever for he is mortal; his days will be a hundred and twenty years."

The *Nephilim* were on the earth in those days—and also afterward—when the sons of God went to the daughters of men and had children by them. They were the heroes of old, men of renown. (Genesis 6:1-4, NIV)

The Hebrew for the phrase "sons of God," *beni elohim*, is used only five times in Scripture—twice in Genesis and three times in Job. In Job, it unquestionably refers to angels: "Now there was a day when the sons of God came to present themselves before the LORD and Satan also came with them" (Job 1:6).

Almost an identical verse can be found a chapter later in Job 2:1. And then elsewhere, the third time the phrase is used it clearly refers to angels: "Where were you when I laid the foundation of the earth? ... when the morning stars sang together and all the sons of God shouted for joy?" (Job 38:7).

While Bible scholars are united in their interpretation of the Job usage of *beni elohim*, they are deeply divided over how to interpret Genesis 6. Generally speaking, there are three major schools of interpreting the phrase "sons of God" in the Genesis passage: 1) It refers to the line of Seth, 2) It refers to kings, 3) It refers to angels. (Walvoord and Zuck 1985, 36)

From my personal experience (interaction with theologians and survey of the literature), the first interpretation is perhaps the most common among conservative, evangelical scholars. The second is considered acceptable, though less common. The third is very uncommon and almost universally derided among conservative, evangelical theologians. The first two interpretations will be referred to as the "non-angelic" interpretation of Genesis 6 in this paper, and the third will be referred to as the "angelic" interpretation.

The Worldview Factor

As this paper will demonstrate, Jewish interpretive tradition of this passage all the way into the first century A.D., and including the New Testament itself, has considered this passage to be referring to angels having sexual relations with human beings. However, today, our Western minds cannot conceive of how this could even be possible. Thus the question begs itself to be asked: Could it be that our interpretation of this passage is more driven by worldview than solid exegesis?

One of our built-in preconceptions in the West is the idea that the "material" and "spiritual" worlds are separate and have little or nothing to do with each other. This worldview assumption has been popularized by the phrase "the flaw of the excluded middle" by anthropologist Paul Hiebert. His thinking on this issue first appeared in 1982 in the journal *Missiology* in a paper called "Anthropological Reflections on Missiological Issues." Since that time his model has become the standard for explaining a major distinction between Western and non-Western worldviews. Missiologist Scott Moreau comments:

> His model was quickly picked up by missionaries and missiologists working among non-Western populations . . . it was used to give legitimacy to demonic and spiritual explanations of phenomena that had been previously overlooked by Western theology, anthropology, and missiology, all of which tended to look for so-called natural explanations for the observed phenomena. (Moreau 2000, 363)

This "flaw" in our worldview has great significance for why we choose one interpretation of a biblical passage over another. For example, conservative theologian Wayne Grudem states emphatically in his book on systematic theology, "Angels are *nonmaterial* beings and according to Jesus do not marry (Matt. 22:30), facts that cast doubt on the idea that 'the sons of God' are angels who married human wives" (emphasis mine). (1994, 414)

Grudem's statement represents what I have observed to be the most common basis for rejecting an "angelic" interpretation of the phrase "sons of God" in Genesis 6. However, not all share this interpretation. I can remember how shocked our Hebrew class was at Talbot seminary when the professor Dr. Richard Rigsby told the class that the Hebrew language and context of Genesis 6 supports the interpretation that the "sons of God" refers to angels. One student was incredulous and asked, "But how is that possible?" referring to the "logistics" of the whole matter. And this seems to be what is driving a non-angelic interpretation. We just can't wrap our minds around how this could even happen, practically speaking.

Dealing with the Two Basic Objections

The first objection to the angelic interpretation of Genesis 6 is that angels are nonmaterial beings. Although this reflects what may be a false dichotomy between what is "material" and what is "non-material," rather than deal with that, which is a larger issue beyond the scope of this paper, it may be sufficient to answer this objection with an anecdote from the Bible itself.

In Genesis 18 we have the story of "three visitors" coming to talk with Abraham. They appear in every way human, but in fact they are two angels and God himself. Not only do they appear human, the text says they have a meal with Abraham: "He then brought some curds and milk and the calf that had been prepared, and set these before them. *While they ate*, he stood near them under a tree" (Gen. 18:8, emphasis mine).

Thus it seems reasonable that if these angelic beings could incarnate themselves to the extent in which they could process food, they could easily go beyond this to possess the anatomy required to copulate with human beings. While this conclusion is based on the assumption that these angelic beings had become incarnate, there is nothing in the text to disprove this assumption, and everything lends itself in that direction. Furthermore, there is nothing ghostly, ethereal, or "immaterial" about these beings. They are presented to us as bodily, physical, and material in every way.

With regard to the second objection, which comes from Jesus' statement in the gospels that in the resurrection we will be "like the angels in heaven" (Matt 22:30), it is important to look at the context in which Jesus makes this statement. Jesus is responding to a question about a woman who had multiple husbands, and the question was whose "wife" will she be in heaven. Thus, the question is not really sexual, but more relational. So Jesus is saying first of all that the angels are "single," not belonging to any particular "partner" but belonging solely to God, as will be the case after the resurrection.

Secondly, Jesus very specifically says, "like the angels *in heaven.*" Jesus is referring to the godly angels whose sole devotion is to God and who serve him in their proper place. Jesus is not making a statement about the *ability* of angels to come to earth in human form and produce offspring with humans. Thus it really is a matter of prooftexting to use this verse to make a point which was not Jesus' point at all.

Making a Case for the Angelic Interpretation of Genesis 6

Jewish tradition clearly supports the idea that Genesis 6 refers to angels in at least two extant accounts. The first is the Book of Enoch and the second is in the Book of Jubilee. Both are very similar in their interpretation. In the Book of Enoch we find a parallel and amplified account of the Flood story where angels are clearly identified as the players in question. The Book of Enoch's extended account is introduced in this way:

> It happened after the sons of men had multiplied in those days, that daughters were born to them, elegant and beautiful. And when the angels, the sons of heaven, beheld them, they became enamored of them, saying to each other, Come, let us select for ourselves wives from the progeny of men, and let us beget children. (Laurence 1838, 5)[2]

The Book of Enoch goes on to describe how these angels corrupted mankind, teaching them astrology, sorcery, and weapon making. Both the Book of Enoch and the Book of Jubilee attribute the corruption that led to the Flood to these "fallen" angels. In fact the Book of Jubilee goes further to say that this corruption extended to all of creation:

> The angels of God . . . took themselves wives of all whom they choose. . . . and lawlessness increased on the earth and all flesh corrupted its way, alike men and cattle and beasts and birds and everything that walks on the earth—all of them corrupted their ways and their orders, and they began to devour each other. ... (Charles 2004, 20)

Both the Book of Enoch and the Book of Jubilee reflect LXX versions circulating in the first century A.D. which translated "sons of God" in Genesis 6 as "the angels of God." (Reed 2005,117) All of this is important context in understanding Jude's statement in his biblical epistle, which says, "And the angels who did not keep their positions of authority but abandoned their own home—these he has kept in darkness, bound with everlasting chains for judgment on the great Day" (Jude 1:5). In a parallel passage, Peter, speaking of the ancient world, writes, "God did not spare angels when they sinned, but sent them to hell, putting them into gloomy dungeons to be held for judgment" (2 Peter 2:3).

Since we know of no other passage in Scripture that speaks of angels "sinning" or leaving their "positions of authority," it seems reasonable to conclude that both Peter and Jude are referring to the events of Genesis 6. Furthermore, since Jude quotes from the Book of Enoch as an authoritative source, we can say with a good deal of certainty that he was familiar with this book's interpretation of Genesis 6 and is even alluding to its more conclusive and amplified rendition of what actually took place. (See Jude 1:14)

While today we may have a difficult time trying to understand how the biblical writers could believe such a thing, we have to remember that their worldview was far different from our own, and much closer to what we find in the non-Western world. Certainly the cultural context of the Genesis account lends itself to an angelic interpretation, as this fits well with other accounts in the ancient world which all seem to be referring to the same event as they do to the Flood, and other common events in Genesis 1-11. *Eerdmans Commentary on the Bible* reflects on this:

> These legends have been traced variously to Persian, Mesopotamian, Canaanite, and Greek sources, with the Greek parallels unquestionably the closest in form, but the basic motifs—gods mating with women and producing half-

breeds; superior beings teaching humanity the arts of civilization in primeval times—are found in mythologies around the world. We have in Genesis 6:1-4, and elaborated more fully in Enoch, the Jewish form of an international myth.... (Dunn and Roberson 2003, 909)

The conservative *Bible Knowledge Commentary* makes the case that the flood was a judgment upon the pagan belief that these offspring were immortal, and worthy of worship. The *Bible Knowledge Commentary* notes that "Pagans revered these great leaders. Many mythological traditions describe them as being the offspring of the gods themselves. In fact bn'lm ("sons of the gods") in Ugaritic is used of members of the pantheon . . . Any superman individual in a myth or any mythology or actual giant would suggest a divine origin to the pagans." (Walvoord and Zuck 1985,36)

This gives the story a very missional purpose in the ancient Near East world. In fact, the entire Genesis 1-11 has a universal dimension, and in every way was intended to be a bridge between the "historical revelation" that every Near Eastern culture (and even beyond) possessed from what was handed down through Adam and Noah's descendants, and the "special revelation" of God's plan of redemption, which we find in Genesis 12. Genesis 1-11 is therefore God's way of connecting every people's story to His story.

Beyond this cultural and missional context, as well the support we find in the New Testament and Jewish Tradition, the text itself in Genesis 6 gives ample support for an angelic interpretation. The key piece of evidence is verse three which says, "The Nephilim were on the earth in these days—when the Sons of God went to the daughters of men and had children by them" (v. 4). Since the word Nephilim in the Hebrew literally means "the fallen ones" it makes no sense to tell us these beings were "on the earth" in those days if we are not dealing with extraterrestrial beings. Furthermore, the text tells us that the offspring of these beings were "the heroes of old"—which links us directly to the oral traditions so common in the Near East about the ancient world that confirm an angelic or extraterrestrial interpretation of Genesis 6.

In addition to all of the above, the angelic interpretation was held by a number of early Church fathers, including Tertullian, Clement, Irenaeus, Eusebius, Justin Martyr, and Ambrose. (Vandekam and Adler 1996, 67) The Jewish scholar Philo wrote a whole treatise on this subject called "Concerning the Giants" in which he speaks of angels intermarrying with humans. (Bamberger 2006, 53) The Jewish historian Josephus also concurred with the angelic interpretation. (Feldman 1998, 22)

Implications for Ralph Winter's Theory

There are three implications for Ralph Winter's theory if we accept the angelic interpretation of Genesis 6. First, it is evident from this passage that angels have the free will and capacity to manipulate God's creation. Second, it is possible that this corruption happened during a definite and limited period of time. Third, when seen in this light, the Romans eight connection, which speaks of creation's redemption coming through the "sons of God," becomes much more meaningful.

Regarding the first, if the "sons of God" in Genesis 6 are angels it becomes clear that these beings have the capacity to disobey God and work against his purposes here on earth. Thus they possess both the ability to manipulate the created order and if they choose, the will to do so. What this means is that angels were given a certain measure of latitude with regard to their activities here on earth, and they are able to use this power for good or evil, just as we are. Furthermore, they are able to "interface" with our world in ways we do not fully comprehend, but would certainly appear to be able to make molecules come together at will to form whatever they so desire (that is if they are able to make human bodies for themselves they can obviously "create" any other form of life they desire as well. Again, this is not *ex-nihilo* creation. It is simply bringing together existing organic molecules to create new life forms, in the same way that our scientists are now discovering how to construct the "building blocks of life" through DNA analysis and manipulation of organic material in laboratories around the world).

This capacity of angels evidenced in Genesis 6 provides a solid biblical and philosophical basis for Ralph Winter's theory that angels could have been agents of intelligent evil design, working to destroy God's creation. Although it doesn't prove that they were indeed acting in this way, it nonetheless provides significant evidence that they certainly could have been.

Regarding the second implication for Dr. Winter's theory, there seems to be the possibility that the angels who "left their positions of authority" and "abandoned their own home" to come to earth have been punished severely for doing so. What this could mean is that the corruption that these angels brought about in creation happened over a limited period of time, and more significantly may not be happening today. That is, what we see today are the after effects of this rebellion. Scripture says that these angels who left their heavenly homes have now been confined to "darkness, bound with everlasting chains" in "gloomy dungeons," awaiting judgment (2 Peter 2:4, Jude 1:6).

Of course, for Dr. Winter the corruption of Creation began at least 500 million years ago. This is based on the appearance of predatory life, which began around this time according to current scientific interpretations of the fossil record. However, without digressing into this debate, what is important to note from the biblical record is that the Genesis 6 account seems to be an explanation for the widespread corruption we find in creation. Certainly that is the way Jewish interpretation thought of it, as is evidenced in the Book of Jubilee. The significance of this is that the Jewish worldview had a concept of "evil" in nature and they attributed this to the influence of "evil intelligence." Furthermore, this corruption of Creation happened during a distinct period of time and those angels involved in doing so are now bound. What this means is that we are now living in an era of restoration and recovery, which will be most fully completed in that blessed eschatological period known as the Millennium. It is here that we see the wolf lying down with the lamb, and the lion eating straw like an ox (Isa. 11:7). In other words, we see a reversal of the corruption that took place. The importance of this is that we have a tradition that rejects the idea that everything we see in Creation today is perfect—or God's ideal. Quite the contrary, we see a worldview that recognizes something evil has invaded the created order. All of this is an important foundation for what Scripture describes as God's redemptive plan for creation in Romans eight.

The third implication of angelic interpretation of Genesis 6 has to do with an intriguing passage of Scripture, which is in every way prophetic—that is it looks forward to something not yet, but shows how what God is doing now will bring us there. The next time the phrase "sons of God" is used in Scripture is by Jesus, who said, "Blessed are the peace-makers for they shall be called sons of God" (Matt. 5:9). The next time after this it is used by the apostle Paul who refers to those who are in Christ and redeemed by the Spirit as being "sons of God" (Gal. 3:26; Rom. 8:14). So what is being described here is an elevation of man to a higher order of creation with reference to the angelic hosts. Scripture says that man was made a "little lower than the angels" (Ps. 8:5). But in Christ we become "partakers of the divine nature" (2 Pet. 1:4), and like the angels, are given the position of "sons of God" in the Heavenly Kingdom.

With this in mind we are ready to examine an amazing passage of Scripture that has direct relevance to this whole issue of the corruption and redemption of Creation. In Romans eight we read that "creation waits in eager expectation for the sons of God to be revealed" (v. 19). We are told that the creation was subjected to frustration, and is groaning as in the pains of childbirth. But God has a plan of redemption through which "the creation itself will be liberated from its bondage to decay and brought into the glorious freedom of the children of God" (v. 21).

These words are pregnant with meaning given the Old Testament context of the "sons of God" rebelling against God and destroying his creation. Now God is raising up a new kind of "son" which is being delivered from the corruption that has come over it—"the redemption of our bodies" as Paul writes (Rom. 8:23). In other words, it is not just the redemption of our souls that God is interested in. There is another dimension to his salvation as well that has a physical—"material" if you will, impact. Thus we are intended to be a kind of first fruits of God's plan to redeem *all* of creation.

Since the phrase "sons of God" is so closely associated with the Flood story, could it be that Paul is purposely using this phrase to link us back with what happened here? What is more, does this passage in Romans give us a glimpse that God may involve these redeemed and elevated "sons of God" in his plan of redemption for creation? That is to say, is it possible that our increased understanding of how life works today, a part of God's plan to restore creation? If evil intelligence was involved in corrupting what God had done, might he be seeking to employ "good intelligence" in correcting it?

From what we know of God he seeks to involve his creation in everything he does. God could have simply built an ark for Noah, for example, but he had him work on it for one hundred years. Our Creator had given mankind, through Adam and Eve, the charge to care for his creation (Gen. 1:28, 2:15). Thus by involving Noah in building a floating zoo, and locking him up with thousands of animals, was he not reminding him of this responsibility?

Could the same be true here with this issue of restoring creation? Is the Great Educator seeking to teach us something by giving us the capacity and thus the moral obligation to do something to fight against evil intelligent design in creation?

This was the fundamental basis for Dr. Winter's theory, and if he is right, it sheds a whole new light on the biblical story from Genesis to Revelation. It demonstrates, first of all, the significance of the physical world in which we live—that it is important to God and he is not done with it yet. He has plans to bring his authority over all things, included the entire created order.

Conclusion

Although there is still much investigation and study required to establish credibility for Dr. Ralph Winter's theory of angelic corruption of creation, scholarship is a house constructed one brick at a time with each piece of foundational evidence leading to the next. Without a worldview change we will never even begin to look for the evidence that is there, or recognize it when we see it. However, if we can establish credibility for the angelic interpretation of Genesis 6, we will have laid down an important "brick" towards not only bringing Ralph D. Winter's theory into the realm of valid scholarly pursuit, but perhaps beginning the first steps towards re-constructing our own Western worldview and bringing it in line with the Bible's perspective. No doubt that was where Dr. Winter was trying to take us all along in the first place.

But even more significant, having established that intelligent evil has invaded our world, it brings greater awareness that Christ's mission to "destroy the works of the devil" extends far beyond what our present mission endeavors seek to engage (1 John 3:8). Only when we realize this can we fully involve ourselves in His mission to see His Kingdom come and will be done *on earth* as it is in heaven (Matt. 6:10).

Winter emphasized this again and again. *There is something here on the earth that God is seeking to accomplish.* Thus we greatly err when we seek to "spiritualize" everything in Scripture that relates to God's dominion being extended over all things. When Paul describes Christ's establishing his reign over every dimension of life, he says "the last enemy to be destroyed is death" (1 Cor. 15:26). Elsewhere he writes that Satan holds "the power of death" (Heb. 2:14). When we read these words what comes to our minds? If it is purely a spiritual interpretation then we have quite missed the full extent of the gospel, for its power encompasses all things, including the very liberation of creation itself from its bondage to the devil and his handiwork. That's what Winter saw, and that's what he tried to get us to see as well. If we can catch only a glimpse of it, we will be well on our way to realigning our thoughts, perspectives and actions with those of the *missio dei* here on this earth, in our generation.

End Notes

1. Wiersbe notes that the word, "giants" in Genesis 6:4 (KJV) is a translation of the Hebrew word *nephilim*, which means "fallen ones." Later translations, such as the NIV, RSV, and NAS, have simply chosen to transliterate the word as a proper noun.

2. This is from the first translation ever done into English of the Book of Enoch. The book was believed to have been lost to history until a centuries old manuscript was discovered in the late 18th century in Ethiopia. Richard Laurence is the translator, who was an Oxford University expert in Semitic languages.

References

Bamberger, Bernard. 2006. Fallen Angels. Philadelphia: Jewish Publication Society.

Charles, R.H.

_______. 2004. The Apocrypha and Pseudepigrapha of the Old Testament. Berkeley: Apocryphile Press.

Dunn, James and John Roberson. 2003. Eerdmans Commentary on the Bible. Grand Rapids: Eerdmans.

Feldman, Louis. 1998. Studies in Josephus' Rewritten Bible. Boston: BRILL.

Grudem, Wayne.1994. Systematic Theology. Grand Rapids: Zondervan.

Laurence, Richard. 1838. The Book of Enoch the Prophet. Oxford: Oxford University Press.

Moreau, Scott. 2000. "The Flaw of the Excluded Middle." Evangelical Dictionary of World Missions, Grand Rapids: Baker Book.

Reed, Annette. 2005. Fallen Angels and the History of Judaism and Christianity. Cambridge: Cambridge University Press.

Vandekam, James and William Adler. 1996. The Jewish Apocalyptic Heritage in Early Christianity. Minneapolis: Fortress Press.

Walvoord, John and Roy Zuck. 1985. The Bible Knowledge Commentary. Wheaton: Victor Book.

Wiersbe, Warren. 2007. The Wiersbe Bible Commentary. Colorado Springs: David C. Cook Publishing.

Winter, Ralph. 2005. Frontiers in Mission. Pasadena: WCIU Press.

Correlation between African Traditional Religions and the Problems of African Societies Today

Chris Ampadu

Chris Ampadu is a WCIU doctoral student from Ghana, West Africa, who studied Sociology of Religion at the University of Ghana. He was a pastor of a Pentecostal church for 12 years and now works with Harvest Foundation to train pastors and church leaders across Africa in the area of wholistic ministry and biblical worldview.

Africa, despite its rich natural endowments, is a continent ravaged with poverty, disease, corruption and conflicts. For years, international aid and development agencies have tried to deal with these problems— with limited success. A predominantly animistic worldview holds sways over the minds of many Africans—a worldview that sees man as a victim of nature, of other people, or of fate. This mindset shifts responsibility for Africa's social ills to the spirit realm, leaving individuals little hope or motivation for working towards a better future.

Even though the church has experienced tremendous growth on the continent over the last two centuries, all too often the church is disengaged from the crying needs of the community— focusing primarily on spiritual concerns. Despite the fact that Christians are the majority in many African communities, poverty, disease, conflict and environmental degradation still abound. The church is often seen as irrelevant by non-believing community members. But the fact still remains that the church is God's principally ordained agency for social and cultural transformation. It is perhaps the single most important indigenous, sustainable institution in any community, with members in virtually every sphere of society (the arts, business, governance, education, etc.). This is particularly true of Africa where statistically almost 50% of the populations (about 400 million people) are Christians and where an estimated four million churches exist.

Yet for the church to effectively advance God's intentions, its leadership needs fresh vision and insight. An understanding of African Traditional Religion is critical in understanding the problems of Africa societies today. Many governmental agencies, including development agencies, non-governmental organizations, multinational and bilateral organizations like the World Bank and the International Monetary Fund, have disregarded the prominent role of African Traditional Religion and have been adopting various economic and political strategies and policies to try to solve Africa's problems. But Africa, with her enormous natural and human resources, continues to be regarded as the dark continent where there are wars, hunger and poverty. In the face of these needs, much of the work of the African church continues to be confined to the area of spiritual things, especially in the areas of deliverance from the powers of devils and witchcraft, healing and saving of souls for heaven—all akin to Traditional Africa Religion. However, the social and physical impact in terms of loving one another and the physical development of individuals and communities has rarely been seen. Large churches have been built and thousands of people go to church each Sunday but transformation of communities has not occurred. Even when people talk about the church, the discussion is typically related only to spiritual issues and all other events and everyday happenings are given spiritual meaning and importance only. This can be attributed to the overwhelming animistic perception in Africa where all natural events are viewed as ordered by the spirits, gods, and ancestors.

Traditional African religion is the indigenous religion of the African before the introduction of any other religions on the continent. It is the aggregate of indigenous belief systems and practices which existed in Africa prior to the coming of Christianity and Islam and to which millions of Africans still adhere covertly or overtly. The term "traditional" is used to refer to the technique of cultural transmission, that is, oral tradition—stories, myths and proverbs—that are used in passing this religion from generation to generation. Beliefs are passed on to posterity through songs, folktales, dances, shrines, and festivals. African scholar K.A. Opoku explains that the term, "traditional" indicates a fundamentally indigenous value system that it has its own pattern, with its own historical inheritance and tradition from the past. "African traditional religion is practiced by millions of Africans in our time and it is therefore a contemporary reality which exists objectively and in fact. It connects the present with infinite time." (Opoku 1978, 9)

This study is to help us to discover what traditional Africans actually believe and to see how these beliefs have inspired their cultures, molded their worldview, and impacted the general development of Africa in the area of hunger and poverty.

Belief Systems

In African Traditional Religion, certain beliefs run through most African societies even though the practices may be different in societies across the continent. A summary of some of their beliefs are summarized in the categories below.

God: In all traditional societies in Africa and in all languages, God is known everywhere as the omnipotent, omniscient and omnipresent supreme being, and various ascriptions and names are accorded to him such as Onyame (the Supreme Being in Akan), Mawuga (The Great God in Ewe) or Oludumare (Almighty, Supreme, in the Yoruba language of Nigeria). He is considered above all beings and things and is considered the creator of all.

Divinities: The divinities stand next in relation to God in the hierarchy of powers. Akans recognize the existence of divinities or deities (*abosom*) as intermediaries between God and human beings and who also derive their powers essentially, from God. They are to serve the Supreme Being in the theocratic government of the world.

Ancestral Spirits: Belief in the spirits of the dead and in their influence over the living is found among all people. It is believed that the ancestors, even though dead, continue to live the same kind of life they led when they were on earth and as such they require food and drink to sustain them, even in their spiritual state of existence. Libation which is the pouring of water, food or drink to the ground is therefore used as a specialized means of communication with the ancestors. These ancestors are not worshipped but venerated.

Spirits: Spirits, according to African beliefs, are omnipresent since they are everywhere at the same time i.e. there is no area of the earth, no object or creature, which has not a spirit of its own or which cannot be inhabited by a spirit. So there are spirits of trees, stones, streams, lakes, the sea, rivers, animals, mountains and hills, forests and bushes, watercourses, birds and other natural objects. Good spirits are thought to bring rain, protection, and birth. Examples of bad spirits are witches, "sasabonsam" (wicked spirits living in the forests), or dwarfs who are thought to be spirits who have assumed human bodies and live in forests.

Religious leaders: Priests of the traditional religions are those who oversee the gods, the prophets, and diviners who do the consultations between man and the gods. They understand the language of the spirits and therefore can foretell future events and happenings. They are the rainmakers who can bring rain in times of draught, the sorcerers, witches and wizards who can cause, pain, diseases and even death to perceived enemies or competitors.

Additionally, the kings, queens and chiefs serve as custodians of the tradition of the people. They usually occupy the 'stools' or 'skins' of the ancestors and therefore are highly respected since they are the traditional rulers and leaders of the people. They are seen as ceremonial figures and are responsible for celebrating the rituals/festivals which maintain the proper relationship between the people, the ancestors, and the universe. They interpret the traditional laws, norms, and practices and receive complaints and petitions. They are seen as the symbols of the community health and prosperity and serve as representatives of the ancestors. They therefore provide a link between the living, the dead, and the spirits.

Wholistic Nature of African Traditional Religion

The African traditionalist is therefore influenced by several forces including God, the ancestors, the lesser gods, spirits and others like witches, sorcerers and magic. According to Opoku, "Religion therefore becomes the root of the African culture and it is the determining principle of the African life. ... It is no exaggeration, therefore to say that in traditional Africa, religion is life and life, religion. Africans are engaged in religion in whatever they do-whether it be farming, fishing or hunting; or simply eating, drinking or traveling, Religion gives meaning and significance to their lives, both in this world and the next."(Opoku 1978, 1).

The African Traditional Religion is very wholistic since it impacts every area of the African traditional life, whether in the city or village, in the office or in the farm, in the building of a structure or in marriage. Prof. Mbiti talking about the African religious heritage says, "Religion is part of the cultural heritage.... It has dominated the thinking of African people to such an extent that it has shaped their cultures, their social life, their political organizations and economic activities." (Mbiti 1996, 10).

Consequences of Worldview

"Ideas have consequences," says Darrow Miller (Miller 2001, 34), and "as a man thinks, so is he" (Prov. 23: 7 KJV). These sayings reflect the truth that a person's (or people's) beliefs impact their attitudes, and their attitudes in turn, impact their behavior, which brings forth consequences (either positive or negative) in their lives. Worldview can be defined as "a set of assumptions held consciously or unconsciously in faith about the basic makeup of the world and how the world works." (Miller 2001, 38)

African culture and tradition cannot be understood and appreciated without looking at the worldview reflected in the religious beliefs of the people. The worldview of a people not only informs what they see, but also it determines the type of societies and nations they build. African Traditional Religion is associated with fatalism, rooted in animism and ancestor veneration. According to Mbiti, animism is the system of belief and practices based on the idea that objects and natural phenomena are inhabited by spirits or souls. (Mbiti 1996, 18) Animists believe in multiple gods which are capricious and unpredictable. For the animist, drought, famine, poverty and hunger are caused by unseen irrational forces. For them the physical world is overshadowed by spiritual realities. To the animist, problems originate from outside, such as lack of rain for growing crops, and therefore to solve the problems of society, the gods, spirits and ancestors must be consulted and appeased.

In these societies, community problems can be traced from the outside rather than internally. For example, instead of a community attempting to find out the environmental practices and attitudes that cause diseases like typhoid, malaria, and cholera, they resort to consulting the gods and appeasing them to ameliorate their problems. They believe that when there is drought or famine the gods must be angry and that these gods are inattentive to the needs of man because of mans' disobedience to the norms and regulations of the gods. The same reasoning applies to infertility of women, famine, epidemics, disasters or any other unfortunate natural events.

In recommending solutions to the total development of African countries therefore, these worldview factors need to be considered. Otherwise, in spite of the best economic, political, and financial measures intended to help solve the numerous problems of Africa, not much will be gained. Instead of looking at the root causes of Africa problems, international donor agencies have typically looked only at the fruits of the problems. Africa's problems include poverty, hunger, diseases, malnutrition, unemployment, HIV/AIDS, malaria, wars and others. If granting of money and offering various forms of assistance could solve these problems, Africa's problems should have been solved by now. But instead, Africa's problems are getting worse. There is the need therefore to look critically at the reason why so many resources have gone to Africa with relatively little impact on the economy or people of the continent. Policies and strategies and proposals that have worked so well in other parts of the world do not work in Africa. Why?

I think the problem lies in the belief systems of Africans since belief systems give birth to the culture of people and culture also determines the attitudes and behaviors of people which in turn determines the laws, education, economics, lifestyle, politics, environment, arts and family life of the people. The African story, or worldview, has been unable to transform our lives as individuals, communities, or nations. The traditional belief system is based on power, control, and fear of death rather than on love, service, and reverence of life.

Correlation between Worldview and Development

There seems to be a close relationship between the traditional African belief systems and the total development of the African continent. Animistic traditional religion believes in millions of gods that are capricious and unpredictable. The gods can be bribed, they can change their mind, and they are very discriminatory and very selfish. As a result, the priests, believers and people of the gods take after the likeness of these gods in their behavior. Some of the elements of this animistic worldview and their potential impact on societal development are described here.

Extended Family system: The traditional extended family system forms the basis of social and cultural life in African traditional religion. The broad network of kinship ties creates uncountable dependents who consistently drain resources such that investment in a viable venture becomes an impossible task for an individual since there are always many mouths to be fed and problems to take care.

Taboos: Traditional beliefs and practices with various taboos and prohibitions prevent production and development of efficient processes. Industrialization and agricultural progress are inhibited by taboos on the use of large tracts of land or forest considered to be sacred or inhabited by gods, dwarfs and other spiritual powers. Nutritional taboos undermine health, especially among women and children. Needed sources of protein are prohibited, such as fish that represent children of the gods and spirits. In some traditional societies pregnant women are not permitted to eat eggs and snails for the fear that their children would develop baldness, and experience copious and excretion of saliva in infancy etc. These taboos result in problems of anemia, vitamin deficiencies, and malnutrition which are injurious to the health and growth of women and the developing child.

Witchcraft: African traditional religionists believe that diseases, barrenness, and sudden deaths are all the works of witchcraft. Such people are not interested in scientific solutions or medical attention since they believe their problems are caused by witches who must be appeased. Due to these beliefs, promoting personal hygiene is a challenge and environmental conditions are a disaster. Preventable diseases like malaria have become the number one killer in Africa, but environmental considerations are generally not pursued due to the belief in witchcraft and magic. Valuable time and money are wasted on measures to counteract the activities of spiritual forces. The fear of witchcraft is so widespread that many people consistently live in fear. This dominant fear seriously inhibits progress and development in communities. Any attempt by persons in these traditional societies to lift oneself above others in terms of good education, business, or even an attempt to build oneself a house will attract the vindictiveness of some of these witches.

Political mediocrity: In the political sphere, traditional religions have traditional rulers who hold all power and authority, assisted by family heads and a council of elders. The chiefs, who ascend to their positions by inheritance, derive their power and authority from the gods, ancestors and the spirits. Even though in modern times a few highly trained people and intellectuals are ascending to chieftaincy, a majority of them are illiterates and do not have the know how to be effective leaders. Some are oppressive authoritarian despots, and enemies of development.

Female Genital Mutilation: The practice of female genital mutilation or circumcision in northern Ghana and other parts of Africa is a grave health hazard to women. (Dolphyne 1991, 37) This traditional practice is geared towards controlling the sexual desires of women and discouraging infidelity in marriage. In this process the clitoris of the female is cut and in some cases, cow-dung or ashes are applied. There is the risk of death from excessive bleeding or infection from the unhygienic methods, and for some women life-long incontinency is the result. But many see female circumcision "as a necessary evil, particularly in those societies where it is a deeply rooted in tradition." (Dolphyne 1991, 37)

Fatalism: The African worldview is deeply rooted in fatalism that says "we are what we are because we were made so and can do nothing about it." This worldview produces a "dependency" mentality—always looking and waiting for solutions outside oneself and not taking responsibility to improve one's circumstance or situation. Such a worldview surely will often lead to underdevelopment because people are not motivated to be creative or innovative, and will not do much to help themselves unless somebody from the outside brings help.

Corruption: One of the causes of underdevelopment is corruption, and indeed Africa is plagued with so much corruption that nearly everybody is involved, including Christians. In some cases, it is actually seen as an abnormality when one disassociates oneself from accepting bribes. In Africa corruption often means getting a contract approved and then doing a job haphazardly because the very officers who are paid to inspect the work are also bribed. For me, this is deeply rooted in African worldview and beliefs since the African gods are thought to be capricious and can be "bribed" through the giving of various forms of sacrifices, offerings or appeasements. Through the giving of "drinks" or some form of sacrifice, these gods can be bribed to kill, spoil, or destroy life or property. Corruption is a problem deeply rooted in the capriciousness of the African gods with the direct result of underdevelopment.

Concept of time: Another African worldview that leads to underdevelopment is the concept of time. This is also rooted in the animistic belief system in which the gods have no respect for time. When they are consulted much time is spent drumming, singing, dancing and incantations before the presence of the gods is recognized in the priests and prophets as they become possessed. This is also seen during festivals when people must drum for a long time before the gods will supposedly come. This worldview has been passed on to the people who do not regard and respect time. A time set at 8 o'clock in the morning might mean a person will show up at 9:00 or 10:00 or sometimes 12 o'clock. This attitude is surely related to underdevelopment because it means that people are paid for what they did not work for or their jobs just do not get done. Benedict Opoku-Mensah recognized this problem when writing in the Daily Graphic of Ghana on June 11. 2008, "the route to a nation's success is hard work, determination, sacrifices, punctuality, and love for one's country. Our poor attitude towards time is drawing our development as a nation backward."

Technology: Animistic beliefs have a great impact on technological development. The African traditional worldview believes floods, earthquakes, drought, and other forms of natural disaster are the physical manifestation of irrational forces. Bad things happen when the gods are angry. With this in mind no attempt is made to find scientific and technological remedies. Instead, the solutions are perceived to lie in constant appeasement of the gods. These are the ingredients of underdevelopment; they are the yeast that helps to ferment poverty and the catalyst that speeds up the collapse of a nation.

Conclusions

In a nutshell, Africa's problems arise from the roots of belief systems which are foundational in understanding poverty and hunger in the midst of abundance and plenty in terms of natural resources. For most agencies, including governments and even mission agencies, the causes of African problems have to do with the visible "fruit problems" that include poverty, hunger, deprivations, malaria, HIV/AIDS, wars, and general underdevelopment. Many measures, strategies, and billions of dollars have been poured into this continent by the West, and yet instead of improving the development of African countries, some are even getting worse. For most mission agencies and churches, the perceived solution lies with evangelism and discipling, which has been taking place for over two centuries, and yet, our problems persist. The majority of believers live in poverty and hunger and some are very corrupt, so that it appears as if Christ came only to save souls and not lives. The solution, in my opinion, can only be found through a critical examination of the roots of belief systems and the lies of the culture that have resulted in enslavement, bondage, and poverty instead of wholeness, dignity, and transformation.

References

Argyle, Eileen. 1958. Religious Behavior. London: Routledge and Kegan Paul.

Arhin, K. 1985. Traditional Rule in Ghana: Past and Present. Accra: Sedco Publishing Ltd.

Asamoah, Ansah. 1996. The Syndrome of Primary Contradiction and Development: The Ghanaian Experience. Accra: Ghana Universities Press. Assimeng, Max.

______.1981. Social Structure of Ghana. Tema: Ghana Publishing.

______.1989. Religion and Social Change in West Africa. Accra: Ghana University Press.

Attagara, Kingkeo. 1968. The Folk Religion of Ban Nai. Bangkok: Kurusapha Press.

Ayittey, George B.N. 1999. Africa in Chaos. New York: St. Martins Press.

Becker, Gary S. 1976. The Economic Approach to Human Behavior. Chicago: University of Chicago Press.

Bediako, Kwame. 1992. Theology and Identity: The Impact of Culture on Christian Thought in the Second Century and Modern Africa. Oxford: Regnum.

______. 1995. Christianity in Africa: The Renewal of a Non-Western Religion. Maryknoll, New York: Orbis Books.

Benneh, G. 1987. Population Growth and Development in Ghana, Population Impact project (PIP/Ghana). Accra: University of Ghana, Legon.

Berger, Peter L. 1986. The Capitalist Revolution: Fifty Propositions about Prosperity, Equality and Liberty. New York: Basic Books Inc.

Bosch, David. 1991. Transforming Mission: Paradigm Shifts in Theology of Mission. Maryknoll, New York: Orbis Books.

______. 1983. "Evangelism and Social Transformation." In the Church in Response to Human Need. Tim Sine, ed. Pages 273-92. Monrovia, Calif.: MARC.

Buconyori, Eli A. 1977. Tribalism and Ethnicity. Nairobi, Kenya: The AEA Theological and Christian Education Commission.

Dube, S.C. 1990. Tradition and Development. New Delhi: Vikas Publishing House PVT LTD.

Forde, Daryll. 1954. African Worlds: Studies in Cosmological Ideas and Social Values of African People. London: Oxford University Press.

Frazer, Sir James E. 1966. The Fear of the Dead in Primitive Religion. New York: Biblo and Tannen.

Gerlach, Luther P. and Virginia H. Hine.1970. People, Power, Change: Movements of Social Transformation. Indianapolis, In: Bobbs-Merill.

Harrison, Lawrence E. 2000. Underdevelopment is a State of Mind. Madison Books.

Harrison, Lawrence E. and Samuel P. Huntington. 2000. Culture Matters: How Values Shape Human Progress. New York: Basic Books.

Hiebert, Paul G. 1993. "Evangelism, Church and Kingdom." In The Good News of the Kingdom. Maryknoll: Orbis Books.

Hillman, Eugene. 1993. Toward an African Christianity: Inculturation Applied. Mahwah, N.J: Paulist Press.

Idowu, Bolaji E.1970. African Traditional Religion. Maryknoll, N.Y.: Orbis Books.

Magesa, Laurenti. 1997. African Religion: The Moral Traditions of Abundant Life. Maryknoll: Orbis Books.

Maggay, Melba. 1995. Transforming Society. Oxford: Regnum.

Mangalwadi, Vishal and Ruth Mangalwadi. 1999. The Legacy of William Carey: A Model for the Transformation of a Culture. Wheaton: Crossway Books.

Mbiti, John S. 1969. African Religions and Philosophy. London: Heinemann.

________. 1970. Concepts of God in Africa. London: SPCK.

Miller, Darrow L. 2005. Against All Hope: Hope for Africa. Phoenix: Disciple Nations Alliance.

Miller, Darrow L. and Stan Guthrie. 2001. Discipling the Nations: The Power of Truth to Transform Cultures. Seattle: YWAM Publishing.

Moffitt, Bob. 1994. Leadership Development Training Program, Levels I and II. Tempe, Arizona: Harvest.

Myers, Bryant L. 1999. Walking with the Poor: Principles and Practices of Transformational Development. Maryknoll: Orbis Books.

Opoku, K.A. 1978. West African Traditional Religion. Accra: FEP International Private Ltd.

Palmer, Jeffery J. 2004. Kingdom Development: A Passion for Souls and a Compassion for People. Chiang Mai, Thailand: ACTS Co. Ltd.

Palmer, Jeffrey J. 2005. Poverty and the Kingdom of God: What in the World is God Doing about the World. Chiang Mai, Thailand: ACTS Company Ltd.

Sachs, Jeffrey. 2005. The End of Poverty: How to Make it Happen in Our Lifetime. London: Penguin Books Ltd.

Seaton, Chris. 1993. Your Mind Matters: Developing a Biblical Worldview of the World. UK: Nelson Word Ltd.

Sultan, Pervaz. 1990. Church and Development: A Case Study from Pakistan. Karachi, Pakistan: FACT Publishers.

Van, Der Watt, B.J. 2001. Transformed by the Renewing of Your Mind: Shaping a Biblical Worldview and a Christian Perspective on Scholarship. Potchefstroom.

Van Rheenan, Gailyn. 1991. Communicating Christ in Animistic Contexts. Grand Rapids: Baker.

Weber, Max. 1958. The Protestant Ethic and the Spirit of Capitalism. New York: Charles Scribner and Sons.

Zahan, Dominique. 1979. The Religion, Spirituality and Thought of Traditional Africa. Chicago.

TRANSFORMING WORLDVIEWS THROUGH THE BIBLICAL STORY

Bruce Graham

Bruce Graham is an adjunct faculty member of WCIU and a member of the Frontier Mission Fellowship of the U. S. Center for World Mission. While serving in India he developed and taught an inductive Bible study curriculum for understanding the Biblical Story and living it out incarnationally among Hindu and Muslim peoples.

The Bible reveals a story. It's earliest chapters trace the history of the people of Israel; it was written to help them understand their unique identity and purpose as a people. Their identity was rooted back in the first human family and the God of Creation who was fulfilling a purpose on earth through them. But Israel is not unique in this sense.

Every nation needs to understand its history and origins. People tell and re-tell their stories, which shape their worldview and identity as a people. But a people's story that is disconnected from God's story will remain hopeless and without enduring purpose. People need to find their place and purpose on earth in light of God's Story and their part in it among the nations.

People filter new information through the grid of their worldview and evaluate it accordingly. In the beginning of the movie *The Gods Must Be Crazy,* a glass Coke bottle is dropped out of a small airplane flying over the Kalahari Desert. It lands among the Sho desert people and awakens intense curiosity. Wondering why the gods have sent this strange tool, they spend several days evaluating its usefulness. Finally the elders conclude that this new thing is not *good* for them, and they set out to dispose of it.

The biblical story is processed in a similar way by people who hear it for the first time. They ask themselves, "Is this *good* for us? Does it give us a better way of coping with our world, of making sense of it? Does this story match reality as we know it? Does it give hope to our people?" For the biblical story to be received and believed by a people, it must *find place* and *connection* within their worldview. If it is perceived as a story that has answer for their people, as a story that fulfills the longings and hopes of their people, it becomes good news to them. They can see themselves connected in a new way to an ancient and holy God that has great concern for them. This God has revealed himself to them in His Son who fulfills ancient promises and hopes for every nation. Following this God will restore their people's identity and purpose on earth. They can become part of God's Story among the nations.

This kind of worldview transformation requires story-tellers who grasp the whole biblical story and can meaningfully communicate it among a people. This is far from bringing a people a new "religion." It is far more than a way to "get people saved." It does not extract a people from their own culture into a foreign community. A skilled biblical story-teller engages a people in a process of discovery that does not disregard their own story, but rather gives them new perspective, new purpose for their people in light of God's story.

Working in India as a teacher of missionary candidates, I observed students learning the Bible by memorizing its details—authors, dates, names of people and places, etc. They learned facts about the Bible and could teach biblical truths. Sometimes people responded, but without foundations in the biblical story, they easily turned to another teaching or another god if something more interesting came along that would meet their perceived need.

But something new began to develop among my students when we began going through the whole biblical story. We approached it *inductively,* seeking to discover God's message within each story. How were the stories connected? What was at the heart of the whole story? Their worldview and perspective began to change. They felt part of what we called then the "Seed-Man Mission" (the term we used to describe the heart of the story from Gen 3:15). They were energized and felt part of something significant.

But knowing the story did not necessarily make them good storytellers. They had to practice telling the story. They had to understand their people to effectively translate concepts and terms in the biblical story among their people. Rather than reading books about the people (usually written by outsiders), we encouraged our trainees to study their people *inductively*. They spent time in teashops and homes, discovering the concerns and interests of the local people. They took part in their celebrations and traditions, always asking God for insight and wisdom that would help them tell His Story more effectively among them.

This led to creative ways of communicating the Story: through song, drama, pictures, or simply story telling, all common forms of expression among Indians. One student drew pictures of successive stories through the Bible, one page per story, and hung them on his living room wall to discuss with visiting friends. Another invited Muslim friends to his home for discussion weekly, and eventually had religious leaders going through the whole biblical story. One woman took months, even years listening to the stories and concerns of Muslim women she worked among. Eventually they began to open up to her, and she had biblical story to share with them that captured their interest. They wanted to hear more.

So, let's multiply story-tellers who understand the whole story. Let's help them internalize it for themselves inductively, so this story becomes their story. Let's encourage them to take the time to know their people and their stories. This enables them to meaningfully communicate and connect God's story to their people's story. For an increasingly biblically illiterate generation, this is going to take some significant work.

INFORMING THE CURRENT INSIDER MOVEMENT FROM THE NEW TESTAMENT HOUSE CHURCH MODEL

Donald Moon

Donald Moon is a doctoral student at William Carey International University, with years of experience as a cross-cultural worker in Latin America. He wrote this paper for the course, Foundations of the World Christian Movement.

T he desire and necessity of meeting together as believers in Yahweh has its roots in the earliest times of the Christian faith. The style of meeting has changed significantly over the years as the Gospel moved into new cultures and as believers found themselves affected by the societies within which they lived, whether from intentional transition to new styles or by force because of persecution or limited freedom. As we consider the situation of people who are followers of Christ but do not embrace cultural Christianity (the insider movement) we must work to understand the dynamics of meeting together in a non-traditional sense and the implications this may have for the future of the church.

Paul's phrase, "Aquila and Priscilla greet you heartily in the Lord, with the church that is in their house" (1 Cor. 16:19 NKJV), gives us a view of what may have been the standard practice of extended families meeting together in New Testament times. We also see this in the history of Cornelius and others (Acts 20:20, Romans 16:5, Colossians 4:15, Philemon 1:2). The practice of making worship, instruction, and fellowship part of the everyday household ritual is promoted in Deuteronomy 6:6-9.

For the first three centuries, Christians commonly met in homes. This may have been due to the lack of an institutionalized faith, the lack of available resources to have a dedicated building, the need to avoid persecution by the Romans or the Jews, the convenience it afforded, or the mobile nature of the members. In order to understand the development of the new Christian movement in the New Testament, it is important that we understand house churches. These churches formed the basis of congregations or fellowships of this new movement outside the Jewish context. They broke new ground in the history of the followers of Jesus as "they both reflected the cultural context from which it emerged and challenged it" (Clarkson, 2000).

In reality, the New Testament model does not concern itself with the actual physical structures where meetings of the followers of Jesus took place, but rather with the nature of the group that met. John Ridgeway states that the Greek New Testament speaks of "the church in the household of so-and-so." However, when this statement is translated into the English, it becomes "the church that meets in the house of "so-and-so" (R. Lewis, personal communication, May 27, 2008). The main principle of the New Testament model is found in the difference between the words house and household.

According to Ridgeway, this translation introduces two changes: first, the word for household (*oikos*), which means extended family, is translated as "house," which implies a building where people live; and second, adding the word "meeting" adds the idea of set meetings with forms that may have been taken from the synagogues (R. Lewis, personal communication, May 27, 2008). Similarly, English versions translate the Greek word *ekklesia*, (which means a gathering of people or assembly, even a random gathering like a mob) into the word "church," which historically refers to a building. The King

James translators specifically chose the word "church" for *ekklesia* instead of "gathering" because King James was trying to oppose independent home gatherings of alternative forms of Protestant believers during his reign. What the Greeks termed as a meeting may have looked very different from what one might normally imagine to be a meeting in a western context. Paul writes in Romans 16:11, "Salute Herodion, my kinsman; greet them that are of the household of Narcissus, which are in the Lord" (Romans 16:11). Tom Neely of the House Church Network feels that the original Greek does not have a separate word that can be translated, "the household." Instead the possessive form of a person's name is used. A literal translation would be, "greet those of Narcissus," or, in other words, "the group that is with Narcissus." (Neely 2007). This reference in Romans 16:11 may have been to a group of unrelated people, but it might also refer to the complete family unit of Narcissus, along with others who joined them on occasion.

In Roman culture, the household was rather extensive and complex. It consisted of several generations and in-laws as well as the current wives, children and slaves. They were all connected and were to be available for the good of the family as a support network. The *patron* was at the top of the structure and provided for the family but also expected their full support. "It wasn't just grandma and grandpa living upstairs, but great-grandfather ruling the roost, along with the subordinate uncles, first and second cousins. This may have been more the ideal than the practice, but as long as that *pater familias* was alive, no Roman could do business in his own name unless the progenitor had emancipated him" (Dupont 1994).

Ralph Winter sees this type of group as a smaller fellowship than that of the synagogue, which was normally made up of ten families. This smaller group may have been created after the divisions in the synagogues that resulted from Paul's preaching (Winter 2008). The idea of a family or household also appears in Acts 21:8-10. The house of Philip seems to have been the intentional destination of those of the new community of faith where they gathered with those of the family and shared their common faith in Jesus. "And the next day we that were of Paul's company departed, and came unto Caesarea: and we entered into the house of Philip, the evangelist, which was one of the seven; and abode with him. And the same had four daughters, virgins, which did prophesy. And as we tarried there many days, there came down from Judea a certain prophet, named Agabus" (Acts 21:8-10).

In reflecting on the expression of faith within a household, Rebecca Lewis makes the following observations: "An '*oikos,*' or family of believers, was likely to express their faith to/with each other on a daily basis at meals, Sabbath celebrations, etc. and to call special times for prayer, as when Peter was in prison and they prayed at Mark's mother's house (Acts 12:12). It was not likely to have 'meetings' as we know and practice in modern house churches which borrow the forms from our regular churches" (personal communication, May 27, 2008).

Local households functioning as a unit and a group of believers were effective in New Testament times for many of the same reasons that they are effective now. The household provides a basic structure of authority and hierarchy that is easily adapted to the formation of a small group. It provides sufficient numbers for interaction, encouragement, community, and fellowship; yet is small enough to allow for individualized attention, support, and accountability. The household provides a physical structure to be used as a place to convene the members of the group. It also provides a natural network of people to whom outreach can take place. This network also provides a connection to the larger society in which, without a proper contact, a person would not be given a hearing. Pierson reflects that it is important to pay attention to the key people such as the heads of households in the social structure in order to be most effective in evangelism (Pierson 1990).

The concept of the household in western societies may be exclusive, limited to immediate family members. However, in today's context in various cultures, the idea of the household is often made up of the extended family including grandparents, parents, children, grandchildren, aunts and uncles, cousins and in-laws. In house church settings, many of these are usually part of the core group. Also, it is very likely to include people from outside the extended family such as servants, employees, friends, neighbors, and other acquaintances. These people may be other families or individuals; while most probably are believers, some may not be.

In my experience in cultures where evangelicalism is tolerated but not necessarily embraced, the idea of having regularly scheduled meetings in a home is a popular method for starting new churches. Usually the meetings follow the form of a traditional church with some minor variations. However, this method involves hosting unrelated people in the home of a believer, which can also have negative effects. While most hosts initially offer their home with enthusiasm as a meeting place, after a period of time the inconvenience of having outside people in the home and the costs that are related with it, begin to cause friction between the host and the group. However, this friction may be managed if the host is the leader of the group and continues to believe that this is a ministry that she or he feels is important to continue.

The model of the household churches in the New Testament can inform the concept of church for followers of Christ outside of cultural Christianity. Lewis expresses that she feels that in true "insider movements" in history, the gospel has flowed through and transformed structures and forms already familiar to that people group (R. Lewis, personal communication, May 27, 2008).

Although one culture may have a form of family structure that is very different from that of another culture, the family structure is something that is familiar to every society and culture. I would suggest that the family structure, or household, can be an effective form within which the gospel can take root and grow as a viable church, providing that key ingredients exist. These ingredients include the following: 1) an authority figure that embraces the gospel, or is tolerant of a member or members of a lower status who does so, and gives his or her support for the member's position, practice, and profession of faith; 2) the basic components of worship, instruction, and fellowship are practiced; and 3) the form and practice that does not run counter to the culture of which the family is a member, but still guards against syncretism.

The gospel affects not just the individual but also those around them. In most cases, this would be their family. All families are not enthusiastic about the changes the gospel brings into their lives. In a country in North Africa, a missionary from South America shares that she is not aware of any church that consists of just one extended family. In her experience, someone in the family becomes a believer and little by little, with time, others join them. But these meetings are with believers of other families. She comments that she also heard of someone who had immigrated to Europe and had later returned to their home country, had shared the Gospel with their family, and fifteen people made a decision for Christ. In this case, she would understand that they would meet together as a family group. Finally, she informs us of a case where one person became a believer and shared his/her decision with his/her family. They are now a group of believers, but a person from Latin America that is leading the group. She shares that while this is type of situation is not common, it is evident that it can be take place. (V. Rosatto, personal communication, May 28, 2008).

Coody's experiences in Kazakhstan show us that meeting people in their homes provided opportunities to share the gospel with people, served as bridges to others, and functioned as places of fellowship. However, he tells us that Kazak villages are close-knit communities, where everyone knows everyone else's business. Word of a community member's faith in Jesus quickly traveled along the friendship and kinship lines. He writes, "the church continued to randomly move from one home to another to avoid detection by the police" (Coody 1998, 101). It is not clear if the communication within the close knit community was a part of the problem of persecution or not. Nevertheless, those involved in an insider style approach to Christian faith in a gospel resistant society would need to carefully consider Coody's experiences. In close-knit communities, testimonies can spread the gospel very quickly, if those coming to faith are not perceived as having become adversarial to the community.

Form and practice also reveal theological understanding. Some might regard the household assembly or fellowship as "churchless Christianity" such as what M. M. Thomas encourages as a "Christ-centered secular fellowship outside the church" (Tennent 2005, 173). With regard to a lack of a visible fellowship that would constitute a church, Tennent writes, "To separate Christian conversion from visible Christian community is to separate two things that God has joined together. The word 'church' (*ekklesia*) in reference to the Christian community was inaugurated by Jesus Christ himself....The very word *ekklesia* means 'public assembly.' The choice of this word helped to launch the church as a visible, defined community into the world" (2005, 174).

While both perspectives emphasize the need for communities to follow Christ, the distinction is that in "insider movements" we see pre-existing communities turning to Christ, while the modern Western church-planting practice has the goal of making new communities by introducing and pulling together into meetings those that are becoming believers (Rebecca Lewis 2009).

The determination that the church be a visible, defined community should not necessarily cause it to be less of an indigenous church. R. G. Lewis comments that "the insider movement promotes the notion that people become followers of Jesus within their context" (2005). He blames the institutional church for not allowing the truly indigenous church to develop and flourish because of the insistence "that people be extracted from their cultural context as they embrace Christ as Lord." He adds, "While it is important that people understand that Jesus is more than a prophet, guru or god, the insistence that seekers throw off the old to seize the new has become a barrier for many" (R. G. Lewis 2005).

However, a household fellowship would seem to fulfill, in at least a minimal way, the role of the church that Lesslie Newbigin describes when he says that the church must involve a visible community. Tennet quotes Newbign as saying that "a visible fellowship is central to God's plan of salvation in Christ; but God's plan of salvation is not limited to the visible fellowship" (Tennet 2005, 173).

The household church is a style of church or fellowship that has existed for millennia. It was possibly the most original style of fellowship for the worship of Yahweh but is not now normally considered as a church style. It has been subjected to both lateral and diachronic change with the introduction of the Jewish tabernacle, temple, synagogues, and western style churches. However, it remains a viable alternative for many, especially in societies that do not embrace Christianity. The challenges to this style of church are many but there is the possibility that this style of "doing church" could effectively be used to transform entire families and, ultimately, societies, through the gospel of Jesus Christ.

References

Clarkson, J. S., (Ed.). 2000. Corinthian House Church Communities. In *Conflict and Community in the Corinthian Church*. Retrieved May 24, 2008 from *http://gbgm-umc.org/UMW/corinthians/housechurches.stm*.

Coody, R. 1998. Fields of Gold. Muncie, IN: Graphics Unlimited.

Corwin, G., and Winter, R. 2006. An Extended Conversation about "Insider Movements." *Mission Frontiers: The Bulletin of the U.S. Center for World Mission, (28)*1, 17-20. Retrieved May 22, 2008 from *http://www.joshuaproject.net/assets/InsiderMovementsRespon se.pdf.*

Dupont, F. 1994. The Household. *The Roman Family.* Retrieved May 24, 2008 from http://ancienthistory.about.com/library/weekly/aa081997. htm.

Lewis, R.G. 2005. Insider movements. *Blue passport.* Retrieved June 10, 2008 from *http://bluepassport.blogspot.com/2005/09/insider-movements.html.*

Lewis, Rebecca. 2009. Insider Movements: Honoring God-given Community and Identity. *International Journal of Frontier Missiology,* 26:1. *www.ijfm.org/archives*

Neely, Tom. 2007. Miscellaneous Writings. House Church Network. Retrieved May 23, 2008 from *http://housechurch.org/miscellaneous/neely.html.*

Pierson, P. E. 1990. Historical Development of the Christian Movement. Pasadena, CA: William Carey Library.

Tennent, T. C. 2005. The Challenge of Churchless Christianity: An Evangelical Assessment. *International Bulletin of Missionary Research, (vol 29)* Issue 4, 173.

Winter, Ralph. 2008. Paul's Middle Missionary Letters: Romans, 1 and 2 Corinthians. Retrieved April 28, 2008, from William Carey International University: *http://www.wciu.edu/foundations_studymaterials.html.*

How Cross-Cultural Workers Choose Their Country of Service: Do We Need a Change?

Dave Williams

Dave Williams (a pen name) received the M.A. in International Development with a specialization in Global Civilization from WCIU. He currently serves in an Arabic-African nation.

One crucial but often-overlooked aspect of taking the good news of the Kingdom to the remaining unreached people groups of the world, the realms of greatest spiritual darkness, is how new cross-cultural workers choose their countries of service. In 1984 statistics showed that 90 percent of all workers were serving in the already-reached parts of the world. (Winter 1984, 321)[1] We need more workers in the places where people seldom feel "called" to serve. Over the past 30 years, as the frontier mission movement has focused on taking the good news of the Kingdom to unreached people groups around the world, the situation has improved slightly.

Dr. Ralph Winter and the U.S. Center for World Mission, along with many others, have called attention to the thousands of ethnic groups yet to have their own church. The Lausanne and AD 2000 and Beyond Movements, as well as Luis Bush's development of the 10/40 Window concept, have impacted and influenced mission agencies, churches, and Christians worldwide to place heightened attention on the unreached peoples of the world. Yet in all these years, the simple idea of agencies assigning new workers to the unreached people groups has somehow been overlooked.

The "Zeal for Me"

In previous mission eras, most candidates simply went to the country where they were assigned by their agency or denominational sending board. Today's self-oriented individualism, however, has resulted in a Christianized form of Maslow's hierarchy with the ultimate goal of "attaining my own personal spiritual fulfillment." (Nussbaum 2005, 40)

Trying to seek our own self-fulfillment, a spin-off of modern psychology, is contrary to the most basic concept that Jesus taught His disciples. "He knew that the only path to true fulfillment lay in denying self. The only way to find truly abundant life is to throw your life away for Jesus' sake." (Hale 1995, 46)

But the "zeal for me," means that the current 6,000 to 10,000 unreached people groups[2] will continue to remain unreached unless agencies change their policies, ask candidates to be willing to go anywhere, and work together with each team of willing candidates (and their sending churches) to research and select an unreached people group.

Why Do Most New Cross-Cultural Workers End Up Serving in Well-Evangelized Countries Rather Than among Unreached People Groups?

The Influence of Short-term Trips

During almost 20 years of mingling with pre-candidates, we have observed that many new cross-cultural workers select their fields of service based on an initial short-term trip where they fall in love with the place and the people, and developed a relationship with a long-term missionary. "Indeed, recruitment is a primary reason agencies began facilitating short-term missions. The Southern Baptist International Mission Board (IMB) appointed 885 new missionaries in 1998. Of those, 85 percent said God used short-term mission experiences to confirm their call."[3]

Deeply influenced by their short-term experiences, new missionaries often choose to go back to serve long-term in the same countries, working with Christians in churches that have already been established. This self-perpetuating pattern is a major factor in keeping the Unreached People Groups from being penetrated.

We must begin to explore both creative and very tangible ways to see the exploding short-term missions movement make a radical shift toward short-term mission trips to unreached people groups.[4] How else will we see a new wave of missionaries who feel "called" to go to these people groups? This will not be easy, though. The first obvious major barrier to seeing short-term vision and pre-search trips to unreached people groups is the reality that so few long-term workers are already serving among unreached people groups. Thus, there are few available to arrange short-term trips. Perhaps we need to challenge, encourage, and train field missionaries on how to organize and host vision and pre-search trips primarily to unreached people groups.

Mentoring by Experienced Personnel

Many new cross-cultural workers expect to have a live person around who can help them at a moment's notice. This is another strong factor enticing new workers to choose to serve in the already reached parts of the world. We must find a better way to pass on crucial knowledge and experience. Many agencies today use email, telephone, and visits by traveling regional supervisors to mentor their people on the field. Sending new workers as teams committed to the same people group will also help with the need for personal contact and encouragement.

The Awe of the Call

In addition to the draw of relationships with workers who are already working in the reached areas of the world, the most influential factor in the choice of a new worker's field of service is what is called one's "calling."

There is a long-standing, hallowed tradition that one must be "called" to serve in a certain country and to a specific kind of mission work. In fact, it seems that most "mission folk" are rather in awe of this mysterious call. If we step back for a moment, however, and realize that the flip-side of our "calling" to missions is millions of Christians who are sure they are "not called," then we may want to go back and re-examine this tradition in light of Scripture.

It is a sad irony that those most devoted to missions are often also the ones most perplexed by the fact that the vast majority of Christians think missions is irrelevant. Perhaps mission leaders, missionaries, and mobilizers have helped fuel this dichotomy between the "called" and the "not called" that is not found anywhere in Scripture. We have been trying for decades to figure out how to get more pew-sitters actively involved in missions either as Senders or Goers. We (mission folk) are sure the Great Commission is a command for all believers, not just those of us who were "called" into full-time mission service. But the very way we talk about our own "calling" may well be one of the prime factors preventing most Christians from having missions close to their hearts. *It is simply too easy for most Christians to say they have never been "called" to missions.*

Perhaps we need to develop a better way of talking about our "callings" with more emphasis on the Scriptures—such as God's command for everyone to be involved in taking the Gospel to the whole world (Matthew 28:18–20)—and less talk about our own personal "callings." Sharing how God is "guiding" us or how the Holy Spirit is "leading" may both be more biblically-based terms. They are certainly applicable in the daily lives of all believers.

Some may argue at this point, "Well that is just semantics; it does not really matter which words you use." (Semantics, by the way, is the study of the meaning of words). The point here, however, is that the images and meanings conjured up by the word "calling" have tremendous ramifications on both new and old cross-cultural workers. We wonder if perhaps individualism and the pursuit of a Christianized self-actualization may also at times be cloaked in the "call" with its focus on *me*, *my* gifts, and *my* desires.

Kevin Howard critiques the traditional biblical support for the concept of a "missionary calling," in his article in *EMQ* in 2003:

> As we think about a calling, let's consider the first missionary journey in Acts 13:2. It says, "And while they were ministering to the Lord and fasting, the Holy Spirit said, 'Set apart for me Barnabas and Saul for the work to which I have called them'" (NASV). The other passage that comes to mind regarding God's call to missions is the Macedonian Call in Acts 16. Paul wanted to preach in Asia, but was forbidden by the Spirit, and a vision led him to Macedonia. Many Christians conclude that all believers must therefore have this kind of clear calling. But, can we make either of these experiences the standard for all other missionaries? If so, why? Nowhere does Scripture promise this sort of clarity when doing God's will. (2003, 462-65)

Howard's article received a strong critique through a long letter to the editor of *EMQ* from a well-known missionary who was "shocked and deeply disturbed" that someone questioned the idea of the "call" to missions service. Few, however, would argue with the concept that the Great Commission indeed applies to all believers ("teaching them to obey everything I have commanded you," Matthew 28:20 NIV). Perhaps if we let go of this tradition of expecting missionaries to have a "calling" we would actually see many more Senders and Goers raised up who are motivated to "send" and "go" simply by obeying the Great Commission.

What we are suggesting is that the "calling" to a particular people group (and country) can just as easily take place after a mission agency assigns the new missionary to a specific people and place. This is simply a timing change.

We believe the Spirit is calling. Yet new missionaries are often not in a position to listen because of what they already thought God told them regarding their country of service. The Bible certainly seems to support the idea of having a willing obedience to God without first having all the details spelled out. Surely flexibility, submission, willingness, and obedience are all qualities that every aspiring missionary should have. Encouraging new missionaries to have a willingness to serve anywhere is not asking them to do anything more than what God is asking them to do. Agencies and sending churches should then work together to assign these willing candidates to unreached people groups.

Agencies Assigning

One of the major reasons for this approach is the fact that mission agency leaders know best where they really need workers (i.e., where no one ever signs up to go). These leaders have access to the latest data on the number of missionaries serving in creative access countries, something hard to get on the Internet or in books such as the excellent *Operation World* by Patrick Johnstone.

Relying solely on God to "call" new workers to the remaining 10,000 groups sounds spiritual and reliant on God. Perhaps agency leaders need to realize that God has appointed them to their position of leadership for "such a time as this." Directing new workers should be the primary function of a mission agency director. Without this broader global vision, new workers will end up making their own private decision based on personal preferences. Likely, the majority will continue to go to the places where many missionaries are already serving.

Pre-Candidate Initiatives

We recognize that it may be many years before the process we are suggesting actually is put into practice by mission agencies. In the meantime we recognize that prospective cross-cultural workers need personal contact as they discern where to serve. We can work to make a way for pre-candidates to have some form of short-term trip as part of their process of discernment. We also want to promote a stepping-stone or interim practice that new missionaries can use before the "waiting and assigning" process becomes commonplace (as we earnestly pray that it someday will). Because so few agencies today are willing to assign workers to specific countries and unreached people groups, we suggest that candidates ask to be assigned to a general region to serve in, move there, and then do field research to look specifically for the people groups with the most need.

My Personal Journey

The convictions we have shared here are the result of a five-year process of discernment about where to serve, as well as almost 20 years of watching others go through the same process. As of this writing, my wife and I, as new cross-cultural workers ourselves, are still open to our agency and sending church to tell us which country and unreached people group to serve in. The long tradition of hearing from the Lord (having a "calling") has been one of the major blocks in our experiences.

For years, we felt led to a T-1 country.[5] When we learned that another couple from our home church was on their way there, however, we were willing to go elsewhere. One day my wife and I were sure that God was telling us to go instead to a T-2 country. The peace and full agreement that we had made us even more sure of our "calling" to the T-2 country. As a result, we prepared for more than a year. We went on a pre-search trip to the T-2 Country, did six months of intensive fundraising, and participated in four months of intensive training.

Just months before our departure to the T-2 country, two leaders in our agency had the courage to approach us and suggest that we not go to the T-2 country because it was one of the "popular" Unreached People Groups, with over 1,000 workers. It was awkward since we were almost ready to leave, but we were willing to follow the guidance of our spiritual leaders.[6] We struggled because of our "calling," but eventually we grew convinced that the opportunity to go where almost no missionaries were serving was really what God had been "calling" us to do all along (Romans 15:20).

We understand why none of these leaders approached us earlier during our five years of searching and seeking where to go. If God had already told ("called") us to go to a specific country, then what leader would feel free to suggest another? The system and current tradition (requiring a "calling") prevented these leaders from telling us where to go since we were so sure that God had called us first to the T-1 country and then to the T-2 country.

God has used our journey to open our eyes to this concept: We think agencies and churches should tell willing applicants where to go, especially to the places where few people ever go. Maybe God has allowed us to go through this wilderness so that we can personally know and understand how so many pre-candidates feel who truly are willing to go anywhere during the discernment process.

End Notes

1. Figure 7 in Winter's article, "The Task Remaining," reveals the situation 25 years ago: 81,500 workers (or 91%) of the mission force serving in reached people groups and only 8,000 Workers (or 9%) serving in unreached people groups.

2. For one of the best brief, yet thorough, explanations on why different groups report different numbers of Unreached People Groups, see Joshua Project, "How Many People Groups Are There?" http://www.joshuaproject.net/how-many-people-groups.php (accessed August 29, 2008).

3. Scott and Sandi Tompkins, "The Short-term Explosion," *Moody* 101, no. 2 (November/December 2000): 14.

4. For more information about short-term and long-term mission, see "The Short-term Missions Explosion."

5. I will use artificial names for security purposes.

6. We believe that only the people who trust God enough to submit to

spiritual authorities (whom they can see) can also be trusted to truly submit to God (whom none of us can see). We believe that emphasizing submission to authority can be conveyed to (and embraced by) Gen X'ers and the next generation because they long to do what the Bible says.

References

Green, Keith. 1982. "Why You Should Go to the Mission Field," *The Last Days Magazine*.

Hale, Thomas. 1995. On Being a Missionary. Pasadena, CA: William Carey Library.

Howard, Kevin.

2003. "A Call to Missions: Is There Such a Thing?" *EMQ*, 462–465.

Johnstone, Patrick. 2001. Operation World. Waynesboro, GA: Paternoster.

Long, Justin. 2006. "Where Are We Going?" *Momentum Magazine*, July/August, 7, http://www.momentum-mag.org/.

Nussbaum, Stan. 2005. *American Cultural Baggage: How to Recognize and Deal with It*. Maryknoll, NY: Orbis Books.

Winter, Ralph D. 1981. "The Task Remaining: All Humanity in Missions Perspective." In Perspectives on the World Christian Movement, ed. Ralph D. Winter. Pasadena, CA: William Carey Library.

International Development without Money? Some Theological Reflections

Jim Harries

Jim Harries, Ph.D., is an adjunct faculty member of WCIU, serving in Kenya in theological education.

The widespread belief that well-being comes from money has distorted Western approaches to meeting human needs. Three alternative goals for international development are considered here from the standpoints of Human Rights and World Religions. The key goal for international development is found to be for people to be brought to a knowledge of and relationship with God.

This article is designed for a particular people and a particular age. Use of English has confined me as an author to certain accepted parameters in Western society, language, and scholarship. I would have to write differently if using Japanese, if confined to the use of ancient Hebrew in the time of Moses, or if addressing slum-dwellers in Cambodia. I consider this article to be a nudge in a certain direction, aimed at a certain people (let us say Western missiological scholars), based on my perception of their current "stand."

How Is Well-Being Defined?

If we presume the goal of international development to be to bring "good" to the people of the world, how then would we define "good"? If good is to be equated with human happiness, then what is happiness? Is contentment more important than happiness? How is contentment measured, or happiness, or well-being? How is poverty measured? And so the questions go on, never seeming to end, and having no clear answers.

Because of the difficulties associated with measuring human well-being as such, scholars have searched for indicators. There are many of these in use, that assess the degree of "development" of a community—such as child mortality, literacy, GDP (Gross Domestic Product), life expectancy from birth, number of doctors serving a given size of community, and so on. If human well-being is put in such terms, then given technology that is known today, improvements in well-being seem to require money. Once the link with money is made, then "money" (and its associated disciplines, accountability and economics) appears to be the answer to everything. Because money is quantifiable and seems to lead to happiness and contentment, supplying money to less developed regions of the world is seen by many as the key to success in international development (as illustrated by Micah Challenge 2007).

This way of looking at international development has become extremely popular in the West for many reasons. It is a convenient way of simplifying complex situations. It is convenient to the West today, because as a result "religion" is made to appear to be a spectator and not a player in the international development game, which obviously pleases secularists. What counts for international development then is getting money and its associated processes, such as technologies, to where it is in the shortest supply. The goal of international development has become that of financial transfer. Jeffrey Sachs has done much to advance this view in his book, *The End of Poverty: Economic Possibilities for Our Time* (2005).

It is almost as if the world stands by in incredulous awe as this money-oriented process continues to charge headlong, as if it could propel everyone to health and happiness for ever and ever, amen! I will not critique this view in detail in this essay, as I have already done so elsewhere (Harries 2006) except to point out what should be obvious—whatever the importance of finances may be in propelling international development, money itself is never sufficient to bring about development. Money has to be used by a complex human being, and *how* that human being uses it is critical to the impact which it will have.

A false confidence in what can be communicated regarding appropriate uses of money, amongst other things, is often engendered by misconceived models of language and communication. I stand with Sperber and Wilson in suggesting that the widely-assumed code model of language has serious problems (Sperber and Wilson 1995: 9). Words do not carry thoughts, meanings, or anything else. Words are mere sounds (or patterns made in ink on paper, or arrangements of electrons) the impacts of which are totally dependent on the mind of the hearer. Words, such as those giving instructions on how to use money, that may be perfectly in tune with one culture and people, may make totally different sense when "heard" elsewhere. This cultural fact is often ignored in discussions of international development.

The Universal Need for Human Community and Leadership

Humans live in communities and have their needs met by other humans. Who is in charge of meeting those needs becomes critical. Hence the major efforts and publicity surrounding the choice of a president for under-developed countries these days, holding democratic (or so-called democratic[1]) elections.[2] Although numerous debates occur at election time, they are condensed into people's preferences for one person or another. If this occurs in national elections, could the same apply at international and / or super-national (or super-natural) level? Is there an inherent human tendency to give "person" priority over other kinds of goals? Do people acting as a society have a track record for naturally following a person who in turn determines their definition of well-being and means of achieving that well-being (or not)?

What if we considered that God has built into the human condition the need for another human to be the ultimate satisfier of needs? Would not Jesus meet that condition, as both fully human as well as fully divine? In fact, the ultimate judge of what is actually "good" for the nations, must be God.

Theology and Worldview Affect Development

The question of the goal of international development becomes a theological question. Theological beliefs affect economic and social states (Weber 1991:251-253). Weber discovered that religious worldviews that reject or encourage escape from the world do not lead their followers to a "rational, methodical control of life" which could lead to economic advance (1991: 270). Key questions about international development, then, are questions about God, his nature, and his will for the human condition. Thus the key to international development is found in theology. While this is denied by some scholarly approaches, it is implicitly acknowledged by others. This is illustrated by the fact that numerous conflicts around the world: between Catholics and Protestants in Northern Ireland, between Jews and Muslims in the Middle East, between Hindus and Muslims in the Punjab, are conflicts between contesting theologies or religious worldviews. It is this sometimes ignored but vitally important component of international development that I want to consider in more detail.

Why focus on issues that appear for centuries to have brought war and conflict, some may argue? The reason, I suggest, is because something that people are ready to fight and die over must be important to them. If it is so important, can scholars afford to ignore it? Could ignoring it lead to disaster? Could it be that a highly "developed" nation without a supporting theology, is like a house built not on a rock but on sand (Matthew 7:24-27)?

People will suffer and die with or without war. One difference is that in the case of war, someone appears to be directly responsible for the suffering. War, murder and killings draw high levels of media interest and public attention, to a degree that other ways of dying do not. Diseases like AIDS[3] cause enormous misery and usually no one can be convicted of murder in the case of an AIDS deaths. Similarly the disasters arising from misdirected international development policies imposed on the poor world by the West go unnoticed, or are covered up. These can be of many kinds, discussed in more detail in Harries (2006). In short, initiators of outside interventions that take away people's control of their own lives (often through financial inducement) are apparently not considered accountable for the messes they make by current national or international law. But messes they certainly do make, that often result in disorientation, confusion and even death. Just as freely available credit can ruin the lives of thousands or millions in the West, so the West's interventions outside its borders have created numerous calamities (Harries 2006).[4] These are the kinds of situations in which a new perspective is badly needed.

Models of International Development

I want to consider three different widely promoted models or ideals of international development in light of the above insights about the important role of theology; that of Christianity, that of Islam, and that of Human Rights. All three are textually based belief systems. All three historically have common roots in ancient Israelite religion. They all interact amongst themselves in complex ways. There is far from total agreement over the definition of each model; so we must tread carefully in comparing and contrasting the three with the ever-present danger that we can over-simplify. The differences between the three are complex rather than objective—as human beings are complex—so must our understanding of necessity be complex. But differences are surely there.

Human Rights

Western Humanists prefer the UDHR (Universal Declaration of Human Rights) to other Scriptures, presumably because it is the most recently devised formula for well-being (1948) (General Assembly 1998a). So it fits with certain Western ideologies—it is individualistic, liberal and secular. In "fitting with the age" however the question arises—what will happen to it when "the age" changes? And the straightforward answer seems to be that it will no longer fit. If this generation thinks that it has, through documents like the UDHR now reached the pinnacle of human understanding and achievement; then it is kidding itself, as did prior generations who considered themselves to be in the same position in their time.

Islam

A large percentage of the world's population prefer the tenets of Islam to those of human rights. It may be true that many of those who prefer Islam have little choice: leaving Islam can result in social isolation by one's family or community; or even in the death penalty.[5] This points again to the importance of correct theology as a goal of international development. Islam arose from dissatisfaction with Judaism and Christianity (Guillaume 1966: 12 and 17-18), and has common roots with them, combined with Arab traditional religion. Muslims consider *their* law to be the ultimate and final—a very copy of an original kept in heaven (Sookhdeo 2001:25). For a Muslim the goal of international development is global Islamisation. As in the case of UDHR above, Muslim scriptures are considered authoritative and final. Also as for UDHR, the authoritative version is considered to be untranslatable.[6] A Koran in any language apart from Arabic is merely an imperfect copy of the real thing.[7] The language in which human rights are defined is clearly English.[8] Unlike UDHR, the Koran is considered to be the outcome of divine revelation. Interpretation, including ongoing divine inspiration, ensures certain degrees of flexibility; arguably more than that of the UDHR; which makes no claims to having a "divine origin." (Hence it attempts to conceal its deep Christian roots.)

Christianity

Christians are, or at least should be, all too aware of some of the failings of the Koran—an aggressive piece-meal reaction to and re-presentation of ancient Semitic, Christian, and Jewish teachings (Morey 1992:107-109). Islam's prominence arose, in part at least, from a weakening of Christianity caused by division and infighting. The Christian Bible, unlike UDHR or the Koran, was not written on one occasion for one generation, but over many years and oriented to many different contexts. Despite the canon being largely closed in terms of content, it is very open to translation and re-interpretation. The prominence of Protestantism has led to a proliferation of translations and interpretations. The Bible continues to be translated and re-translated into numerous languages—not as "copies" of the "real thing" (as would be the case with the Koran) but every time as fully inspired. As much of the rest of the Bible itself can be considered a commentary on the words of Moses (the Pentateuch), so numerous texts are a part of that still ever-expanding literature—including ancient Jewish writings such as the Talmud, writings of the church fathers, Augustine, church councils, right up to devotional books produced in contemporary times. Even the Koran and the UDHR itself are in a sense all later interpretations of the Bible. So the question can be asked— is the goal of international development to achieve allegiance to only small parts of an ancient heritage that ignores most of its roots (UDHR and Islam), or is it to enable the globe to benefit from the whole gamut of God's intentions for the world?

Interpretation—the Key

It should be clear that no authoritative text can survive through many generations without being either re-interpreted, or re-written. Important questions therefore regard the re-interpretation process.

Let as take an example from the UDHR. As it stands it strongly promotes education (General Assembly 1998), but it does not specify in which language education is to be conducted. This has resulted in one people's educational system (Westerners') being spread around the globe in one language. While this may be of enormous benefit to the people concerned (native English Speakers) in bringing the world into their service, it may hamper the prospects of education developing independently or addressing peculiar contexts not found in the native English speaking world. In due course, a stipulation is likely to be added to the UDHR, that the education children receive should be in a language that they understand. Such addition is the kind of 're-interpretation' that I am referring to.

If UDHR is open to such amendments, then one must question its universality. (If not, then, one must question its flexibility!) If the course of time requires such 'amendments' (or re-interpretations), as has always been the case for every other text in the world (classically the Law of Moses), then the same will apply to UDHR. But then, if the passing of time forces amendments and re-interpretations, how can one be certain that one text is valid inter-culturally? That is—if shifts in (say) Western culture require re-interpretation of authoritative texts, do the simultaneous differences *between peoples* around the world not imply that particular interpretations of UDHR were never universal in the first place? Perhaps the UDHR is best understood as just another of many texts arising in the Judeo-Christian tradition that will have their place in history like any other. If so, then it ought not be given a singular status as universal. And if the UDHR is not "universal," then how and where is it to be applied? Can it then legitimately be the goal of international development?

Sanneh points to significant differences in acceptable means of interpretation between the Bible and the Koran, because the true Koran is only legitimate in one language, namely, Arabic (Morey 1992:117). But does confinement to one language (Arabic) in one written text (the Koran[9]) mean that Islam is unchanging? It would seem hardly so—as generation follows generation, Arabic as any other language will be used differently, so the Koran will be interpreted differently. Confining legitimate re-interpretation through the use of one language cannot mean that the interpretation of the Koran never changes, but rather that Sunni Islam (at least[10]) is tied to the whim of certain native Arabic speakers. That is, that "prescriptive authority" is given to relatively few experts so, in Sanneh's words "Arabic acts to disenfranchise the vernacular" (1989:212).

While the current internationalization of English may be threatening to do the same for the Christian church's Scripture, the Bible, the inherent and widely accepted translatability of the Bible acts against the likelihood of authoritarian control. Even the Hebrew Bible (Old Testament) Jesus used was after all a translation (the Septuagint—a translation from Hebrew into Greek). The Bible retains manifold possibilities of re-interpretation, which have contributed to the kind of diversity that has long been a feature of the Christian church.

Understandings of God in Relation to the Goal of International Development

The above discussion, although of necessity brief and simplified, has considered three contemporary contenders for the role of 'goal' of international development, from the point of view of history, flexibility, universality, and ease of re-interpretation. This approach has made implicit theological assumptions. It has assumed that God exists, that he is concerned for mankind, and that therefore it is in mankind's interests to seek to pay attention to him. Those who do not share such assumptions may struggle with the arguments presented. Unlike much recent scholarship, I do not consider secularism (the theory of natural evolution, the materialist worldview etc.) to have privileged status—so my assumption are as or (I would argue) more valid than those, for example, that underlie science.

Questions on international development often implicitly concern the role of international aid-flows and transfer of science and technology. An appropriate Christian theological view of such is a part of the wider theological project. The Biblical emphasis would seem to be on *enabling* people, especially by setting them free (Luke 4:18-19) from what is evil and untoward (such as demons, e.g. Luke 4:18-20) and not on providing them with money.

By way of conclusion, I submit that the goal of international development should be to bring people to a knowledge of and relationship with God, as he is known through his Son Jesus who came to the world in human form, guided by followers of Jesus who are led by God's Spirit, as outlined in the Christian scriptures, and considered in contemporary contexts.

End Notes

1. Many questions have been raised as to whether African countries can have 'true democracy', especially following recent elections in Kenya and Zimbabwe. See Muhammad (2008) and Nation (2008): "The conduct of the 2007 elections [in Kenya] was so materially defective that it is impossible ... to establish true or reliable results for presidential or parliamentary elections" citing an official report.

2. As I write in 2008 the Kenyan, Zimbabwean and especially American elections are taking up enormous amounts of media attention, and the focus in each case is strongly on choice of President.

3. I understand that technically AIDS is not a disease, but a state of increased vulnerability to disease.

4. I give three simple examples. One, the attack on traditional "courting" systems combined with promotion of condoms in Africa that has resulted in promiscuity which, combined with AIDS, has caused enormous suffering and early death. Two, encouragement of democracy which implies majority rule in Rwanda, that contributed to the massive genocide of 1994. Three, untold church splits in Africa arising from

disputes over donor money and relationships with Westerners.

5. "In Islam all schools of law *(madhhahib)* agree that adult male apostates from Islam should be killed" (Sookhdeo 2007).

6. I suggest that the UDHR is considered 'untranslatable' because it is implemented internationally without consideration of linguistic and cultural differences. At least in much of Africa, "rights" are a foreign import and applied according to Western values (and linguistic / cultural presuppositions) – not indigenous African values and standards.

7. Illustrated by Sanneh by recounting the opposition met by an attempt to translate it to Hindi (Sanneh 1989: 211).

8. As far as East Africans are concerned. An accomplished Kiswahili speaker reading the Kiswahili version (General Assembly 1998b) easily discovers that it is a translation from English, and rooted in Western and not East African values.

9. I am for purposes of this essay ignoring the *hadith* and other guiding texts of Islam that may be more 'flexible" than the Koran itself.

10. Sunni Islam is more closely tied to a 'literal' interpretation of Islam than are Shia Muslims (Sookhdeo 2001:66).

References

General Assembly. 1998a. "Universal Declaration of Human Rights." http://www.un.org/Overview/rights.html (accessed 24.09.08)

General Assembly. 1998b. 'OHCHR: Swahili/Kiswahili () - Universal Declaration of Human Rights.' http://unhcr.ch/udhr/lang/swa.htm (accessed 24.09.08)

Guillaume, Alfred.1966. Islam. Middlesex: Penguin Books Ltd.

Hands, Greg, MP. 2008. "Doing Something about Britain's Personal Debt Crisis – by Greg Hands MP." http://cornerstonegroup.wordpress.com/2008/02/28/doing-something-about-britain%E2%80%99s-personal-debt-crisis-%E2%80%93-by-greg-hands-mp/ (accessed 24.09.08)

Harries, Jim.2006. "The Immorality of Aid to the 'Third World'." http://www.jim-mission.org.uk/articles/aid.htm (accessed 4.02.07)

Micah Challenge. 2007. "Halfway Isn't Far Enough." *Idea* May/June:10.

Morey, Robert. 1992. The Islamic Invasion: Confronting the World's Fastest Growing Religion. Eugene, Oregon: Harvest House Publishers

Nation. 2008. "Polls: We Will Never Know the Winner. Kriegler reports it is impossible to Say Who Won race for State House." *Daily Nation*. Thursday, September 18th, p. 1.

Muhammad A. Akbar. 2008. "'Democracy' Fails Africa." http://www.finalcall.com/artman/publish/article_4414.shtml (accessed 24.9.08)

Nickle, Keith F. 1966. The Collection: a Study in Paul's Strategy. Illinois: Allec R. Allinson Inc.

Plantinga, Alvin. 1983, "Reason and Belief in God." In: Plantinga, A., and Wolterstorff N., (eds.) Faith and rationality: reason and belief in God, pp. 16-93. London: University of Notre Dame Press

Sachs, Jeffrey D. 2005. The End of Poverty: Economic Possibilities for Our Time. New York: Penguin Books.

Sanneh, Lamin. 1989. Translating the Message: The Missionary Impact on Culture. New York: Orbis Books

Sookhdeo, Patrick. 2001. A Christian's Pocket Guide to Islam. Ross-shire, Scotland: Christian Focus Publications.

Sookhdeo, Patrick. 2007. "Islamic Teaching on the Consequences of Apostasy from Islam." http://www.barnabasfund.org/News/archives/article.php?ID_news_items=295 (accessed 24.09.08)

Sperber, Dan, and Deirdre Wilson. 1995. Relevance: Communication and Cognition (second edition). Oxford: Blackwell.

Weber, Max. 1991. The Sociology of Religion. Boston: Beacon Press

SHALOM: THE GOAL OF THE KINGDOM AND OF INTERNATIONAL DEVELOPMENT

Beth Snodderly

The Editor concludes this collection of WCIU faculty, student, and alumni articles with a biblical perspective.

The Kingdom of God is ... righteousness, peace, and joy (Romans 14:17).

They made my brother hold a flashlight and watch while they took turns raping me. They were like animals. When he refused their order to rape me, they stabbed him to death in front of my eyes, just as they had done with my parents a year ago."

For eight months this Congolese woman was a slave to the Congolese rebel army, raped multiple times every day, until she finally managed to escape. Reunited with her children, whom she had thought dead, she is now raising her new baby, Hope, the child of one of her rapists, while she participates in a job training program designed for women like herself. This woman's plight is common in the Congo, where in some rural villages 90% of the women have been raped, ages 3 to 73. The only doctor in the only hospital on the "front lines" of this civil war, who does his best to repair torn and broken bodies, is the only man the women who come to him have been able to trust. Their husbands often leave them, this doctor recognizes, because they have been humiliated by being powerless to defend their women.

In a resource-rich country, this systematic destabilization of the society through violent acts against the women, enables certain interest groups to rape the natural resources of the land for their own benefit. [1]

The Need for Shalom

Compare the condition of this society to that described by the prophet Isaiah in 59:4-11: No one calls for justice; no one pleads his case with integrity. ... They conceive trouble and give birth to evil. ... Their deeds are evil deeds, and acts of violence are in their hands. Their feet rush into sin; they are swift to shed innocent blood. Their thoughts are evil thoughts; ruin and destruction mark their ways. The way of peace they do not know; there is no justice in their paths. They have turned them into crooked roads; no one who walks in them will know peace. So justice is far from us, and righteousness does not reach us. We look for light, but all is darkness; for brightness, but we walk in deep shadows. Like the blind we grope along the wall, feeling our way like men without eyes. At midday we stumble as if it were twilight; among the strong, we are like the dead. ... We look for justice, but find none; for deliverance, but it is far away.

Questions

1. What is wrong with these two societies? How do societies get to the place where such unrestrained violence and corruption break out?

2. What does God want human life to look like?

3. What are the essential conditions for a society to experience wholeness, peace and safety?

4. What is the responsibility of the body of Christ to those in harm's way? What should be the role of Kingdom-minded workers in addressing the roots of human problems around the world and what opposition should they expect to face?

Shalom Word Study

Before setting out to "solve" the problems of the world it is important to know the goal toward which one is working. What does God want human life to look like? One way to approach answers to that question, and the others above, is to survey the connotations of the Hebrew word, "*shalom*," commonly translated "peace," but which implies much more: wholeness and wellness in the context of right relationships with God, people, and nature. This article seeks to further the understanding of what it means to see the advance God's Kingdom, through a survey of the context of the occurrences of the word, "*shalom*," in the Old Testament, with some comparisons to the New Testament. The usage and context of several Greek words for "*shalom*" that were used by the translators of the Septuagint, will be the basis for this study. (See a comprehensive list at the end of this article, "*Shalom*: Right Relationships with God, People, and Nature.") The descriptions of *shalom* will be seen to correspond with descriptions of God's will for people and all creation. But there is an enemy actively opposing God's will. The theme of the Bible is the battle for the rulership of this world. In John 12:31 Jesus says of his upcoming death, "now the ruler of this world is being driven out." A summary in 1 John 3:8 of the purpose of Jesus' appearing on earth says, "the Son of God came to destroy the works of the devil." Those who participate with the Son of God in this battle will face the conditions the enemy seeks to impose: "the whole world lies in the power of the evil one" (1 John 5:19). The plight of those lying in the evil one's power are described in the Old Testament, although the enemy's presence was not well recognized, in passages where the opposite of *shalom* is described.

Descriptions of the Absence of Shalom

Question 1. What is wrong with these two societies? How do societies get to the place where such unrestrained violence and corruption break out?

Many of the occurrences of the term, *shalom,* in the Old Testament are in the context of conditions in which peace, safety and well-being are absent. These passages describe the opposite of God's will and illustrate principles for understanding what has gone wrong in societies experiencing violence and danger.

• *God judges evil societies*

Old Testament history shows that God turns his back on those who do evil. He allows evil societies to be overthrown and destroyed, whether by the violence of other evil societies or by natural disasters, or both (see Jeremiah 33:4-6 and 4:22-26). Ralph Winter has commented that it shows God's commitment to free will that innocent people and even believers suffer while God is allowing evil cultures and societies to burn themselves out and destroy one another.[2] Jeremiah pointed out to the people of Jerusalem, regarding the disasters and lack of *shalom* he prophesied were coming to them, "Your own conduct and actions have brought this upon you. This is your punishment" (4:18).

• *God deals with societies according to their own standards*

In a land full of violence, God said he would deal with the people according to their conduct and judge them by their own standards (see Ezekiel 7:23-27). In seeking to understand the judgment of God against a society, questions such as these might be helpful:

What signs can be found in the history of the society of God's activity or redemptive analogies?

In what ways have the people, particularly the leaders, disobeyed and rebelled against what was right according to their own culture's traditional values?

What are the society's own expectations of justice and judgment?

• *Nature is cursed when a society turns away from God*

A person or group that presumes to think they are "safe and blameless" (Hebrew: *shalom*/ Greek: *hosia*) when in reality they are persisting in going their own way, contrary to God's way, will bring disaster on the land. "All the curses written in this book," listed in Deuteronomy 28:15ff, will come against that person or society, Moses warned (see Deut. 29:18, 19). Among the curses for those not following God's commands are "wasting disease, with fever and inflammation, with scorching heat and drought, with blight and mildew, which will plague you until you perish" (Deut. 28:22).

Descriptions of the Presence of Shalom

Question 2. What does God want human life to look like?

In contrast to the descriptions of the absence of *shalom*, descriptions of the presence of *shalom* illustrate God's will for people and the land. In a presentation to the staff of the U.S. Center for World Mission on February 14, 2008, Paul Pierson asked the question, "What does God want human life to look like?" He answered his own question with a good description of *shalom*, which is also a good description of the goals of Kingdom mission: grace, health, education, safety, well-being for all people.

These qualities flow from being in right relationship with God, as seen in Jeremiah's prophecy that tied the concept of "prosperity" (Hebrew: *shalom*/ Greek *eirene*) to God's forgiveness of sins of rebellion. "I will ... forgive all their sins of rebellion against me. Then this city will bring me renown, joy, praise and honor before all nations on earth that hear of all the good things I do for it; and they will be in awe and will tremble at the abundant <u>prosperity and peace</u> I provide for it" (33:8, 9).

From this passage, it is clear that *shalom* is a quality that is observable. A visible evidence of *shalom* in the realm of nature was understood by one of Job's comforters as including the wild animals being at peace (Hebrew *shalom*/ Greek *eirene)* with humans (Job 5:24). Isaiah elaborated on this concept in describing the reign of the Messiah: "The wolf will live with the lamb, the leopard will lie down with the goat, the calf and the lion and the yearling together; and a little child will lead them. ... They will neither harm nor destroy on all my holy mountain, for the earth will be full of the knowledge of the Lord as the waters cover the sea" (11:6, 9).

In his list of animal life that will no longer harm or destroy when the Lord's *shalom* is being experienced, Isaiah's lack of knowledge prevented him from including harmful micro-organisms that cause disease in humans, animals, and plants. But knowing in the 21st century that disease is caused by bacteria and viruses, and knowing that disease is one of the curses that is an evidence of the lack of *shalom* (see Deut. 28:22 and Jer. 32:23), it seems reasonable to include the "taming" (or eradication) of these types of "animal" life in a contemporary application of the understanding of *shalom*. This is a frontier of Kingdom mission that missiologist Ralph Winter strongly urges in order to glorify God by making known to the world that He is not the author of disease and suffering.

Rather, God's will is demonstrated by another observable sign of *shalom*: health and healing. To a formerly wicked city and the people in it, God says through the prophet Jeremiah, "I will bring health and healing to [the city]; I will heal my people and will let them enjoy abundant peace/*eirene* and security (Greek *pistin*—the root word for faithfulness)" (Jer. 33:6). This passage demonstrates that there is no dichotomy between social and spiritual healing or between physical and spiritual healing. *Shalom* is holistic.

Conditions for Experiencing Shalom

Question 3. What are the essential conditions for a society to experience the wholeness, peace and safety described in these passages of Scripture?

When a society repents and turns to God, Scripture shows, He is willing to restore and bless the people with *shalom/eirene* (see Ps. 30:11; Jer. 33: 6, 9). A concordance study shows there seem to be two conditions for a society or person to experience *shalom*. One is the intention to follow God's laws and principles. The other is acceptance of God's provision of a substitute punishment for *not* following God's laws and principles. In both cases opposition should be expected from the enemy whose goal is the opposite of God's will.

1. The principle of keeping God's requirements as a condition for blessing and *shalom* was specifically stated to Isaac shortly before he encountered Abimelech, king of the Philistines (see Genesis 26:1-5). It is through following God's guidelines that a society can function well. In fact, all nations on earth willing to function according to the will of God as revealed through His chosen people, will end up being blessed materially and spiritually (*shalom*). This is seen in Genesis 26:4, 5 where God repeated the promise to Isaac that was originally given to Abraham: "through your offspring all nations on earth will be blessed, because Abraham obeyed me and kept my requirements, my commands, my decrees and my laws." Immediately following this promise is an illustration of one of the nations, the Philistines, being blessed by the presence of Isaac's family, in spite of various problems, and sending him away in peace/*shalom*/*eirene* (Gen. 26:29, 30), without further quarreling or fighting.

When God's principles are followed, peace results. This is also seen in the encounter between Moses and his father-in-law. Jethro showed Moses how to satisfy the peoples' need for justice, without wearing himself out, by delegating some of the work to others. Jethro specifically stated that if "God so commands" that the principles of delegation be followed, and if Moses did follow them, then Moses would be able to stand the strain of leadership and the people would go home satisfied (*shalom*/"in peace"). (See Exodus 18:7-23.)

But *shalom* does not come easily. A spiritual enemy has it as his goal to prevent *shalom*; to prevent God's will from being done. Broken relationships among people and with God characterize the activities of people and nations throughout the Old Testament. A pattern seen throughout the Major and Minor Prophets is the repeated description of God allowing one nation to punish another for their evil ways, with the focus on the people of Israel and Judah who had the most opportunity to know God's expectations, yet failed to follow Him. As God would withdraw His presence and hand of protection, the evil one, the "ruler of this world" (John 12:31) would step in and create havoc. The Old Testament prophets, without specifically acknowledging this enemy, recognized that God was somehow using or allowing one evil nation to punish another. Then the instrument of punishment of one group of people would in turn experience punishment for their own evil ways, in a seemingly never-ending cycle. (See, for example, Hosea 8:3-8; Joel 3:1-7.)

But a climactic statement by the prophet Isaiah points toward the possibility of a break in this vicious cycle. Speaking of the coming Messiah, Isaiah prophesied: "He was pierced for our transgressions, he was crushed for our iniquities; the punishment that brought us <u>peace</u> (*shalom/eirene*) was upon him, and by his wounds we are healed" (Is. 53:5). Jesus brought an end to the cycle of one society punishing another for the evils it commits in its rebellion against God. Jesus took the final punishment on behalf of any person or society that will accept his peace offering. This was the defeat of the evil one's schemes against humanity (1 John 3:8—"the Son of God appeared to destroy the works of the devil"). By accepting this substitute punishment, people and societies can break out of a vicious cycle and experience healing of broken relationships with God, people, and nature.

The Battle for Shalom

Question 4. What is the responsibility of the body of Christ to those in harm's way? What should be the role of Kingdom-minded mission workers in addressing the roots of human problems around the world?

Jeremiah seemed to be saying, in his plea to Israel, that if God's people will obey him, the rest of the world will be blessed: "If you put your detestable idols out of my sight and no longer go astray, and if in a truthful, just and righteous way you swear, 'As surely as the Lord lives,' then the nations will be blessed by him and in him they will glory" (4:1,2). The challenge to be God's obedient people, who are experiencing some of that blessing, becomes very personal if we dare to ask ourselves the question from the Lord through the prophet Haggai: What are we doing building our paneled houses and elaborate landscapes when God's "Temple," the intended Body of Christ, is in shambles around the world? (see Haggai 1:3); when there are people from many nations in harm's way whom God wants to redeem for his glory (Is. 11:9)? What is the part of 21st-century believers in the battle for the planet?

Quoting again from Paul Pierson's presentation on February 14, 2008, "we are called to call people to become followers of Jesus as authentic disciples of Jesus in their culture and to show something to the world of what the Kingdom of God means, and what are its values." Pierson added, "What passion has God given you? If he gives you a passion He'll give you the gifts to go with it."

The Body of Christ contains people with the gifts to "do" or "make" *shalom* in many different areas: justice, peace-keeping, skill-building for economic independence, health, fighting and eradicating disease, etc. All of these peace-making activities can potentially demonstrate the values of the Kingdom and bring *shalom* into the lives of troubled people and societies. Jesus concluded his farewell speech to his disciples by promising *shalom* in the midst of trouble: "I have told you these things, so that in me you may have peace/*eirene*. In this world you will have trouble. But take heart! I have overcome the world" (John 16:33). In 1 John we see that believers in Jesus also overcome the world and the evil one who rules it (1 John 2:13, 14; 5:4). As a result they are able to enjoy and pass on to others the *shalom* of God, as seen in the greetings of 2 John and 3 John. Compare the Greek words in these greetings with the list of words found at the end of this article showing how the Septuagint translated *shalom*:

"Grace/*charis*, mercy/*eleos* and peace/*eirene* from God the Father and from Jesus Christ, the Father's Son, will be with us in truth and love" (2 John 3).

"Dear friend, I pray that you may enjoy good health/*hugiainei* and that all may go well with you, even as your soul is getting along well" (3 John 2).

Concluding Challenge

What will it take for a society that is not enjoying "good health," that is engulfed in evil and experiencing the absence of God's presence, to get to the place where it experiences *shalom*? What would *shalom* look like in the Congo, in Sudan, in Iraq, in Myanmar? Contrast the unjust and violent conditions in such societies with Zechariah's prophesy, as he sings and prophesies to his baby son, John the Baptist, in Luke 1:68-79:

> Praise be to the Lord, the God of Israel, because he has come and has redeemed his people.
>
> He has raised up a horn of salvation for us in the house of his servant David (as he said through his holy prophets of long ago),
>
> salvation from our enemies and from the hand of all who hate us—to show mercy to our fathers and to remember his holy covenant, the oath he swore to our father Abraham:
>
> to rescue us from the hand of our enemies, and to enable us to serve him without fear in holiness and righteousness before him all our days.
>
> And you, my child, will be called a prophet of the Most high: for you will go on before the Lord to prepare the way for him,
>
> to give his people the knowledge of salvation through the forgiveness of their sins, because of the tender mercy of our God,
>
> to shine on those living in darkness and in the shadow of death, to guide our feet into the path of <u>peace</u>/*eirene*.

Zechariah sang about salvation from human enemies, about serving God without fear in holiness and righteousness, forgiveness, mercy, peace—the same *shalom* spoken of throughout the Old Testament. In the context of similar justice, righteousness and faithfulness, Isaiah described "salvation" from feared enemies in the realm of nature (which can also represent disease micro-organisms that were unknown at that time): "The wolf will live with the lamb, the leopard will lie down with the goat, ... and a little child will lead them. They will neither harm nor destroy on all my holy mountain, for the earth will be full of the knowledge of the Lord" (Is. 11:6, 9).

In the holistic nature of *shalom,* there is no dichotomy between physical and spiritual health and well-being. *Shalom* is the description of God's will for the earth and everything living in it. *Shalom* is the goal of God's Kingdom: "Our Father in heaven ... your kingdom come, your will be done on earth as it is in heaven" (Matthew 6:10). Believers need to be ready for serious opposition in the spiritual battle for the rulership of this world. Jesus came and "made peace" by his death on the cross. Believers should expect no less opposition than he faced when they join him as "sons of God" in making (waging) peace in a broken war-torn world.

"Blessed are the peacemakers for they will be called sons of God" (Matthew 5:9).

Shalom: Wholeness and Right Relationships with God, People, and Nature

Occurrences and Usage in the Septuagint of the Greek Words Used to Translate the Hebrew, Shalom

hugiainei 10x

Wellness, physical health Gen. 29:6; 37:14; 43:27,28; 2 Sam. 20:9; Esther 9:30; Is. 9:6

Greeting (I wish you well, peace to you, good health to you, prosperity to you) Ex. 4:18; 1 Sam. 25:6

Farewell (go in peace/health)   2 Sam. 15:9

sotarias 3x

Safety ("salvation") Gen. 26:31; 41:16; 44:17

hileos 1x

God deal mercifully with you, fear not Gen. 43:23

hosia 1x

Let good happen to me Deut. 29:19

anepause 1x

God has given me rest round about (no one is plotting against me) 1 Kings 4:24

euthenousi 1x

Their houses are safe (good condition; no rod of punishment from God is upon them) Job 21:9

chairein 3x

No joy to the wicked Is. 48:22; 57:21

Go out with joy, and be led forth with peace/gladness Is. 55:12

teleian 1x

Wholly carried away (Hebrew: peacefully exiled) Jer. 13:19

eirenes 169x

Peaceful Gen. 15:15; 2 Kings 22:20; 2 Chron. 34:28; Jer. 34:5

Endnote

1. Summary of a "60 Minutes" segment, televised in the summer of 2008.

2. Comment in a private conversation with the author on February 14, 2008.

www.ingramcontent.com/pod-product-compliance
Lightning Source LLC
Chambersburg PA
CBHW051114050726
47592CB00002B/817